Also available in this series (titl

Interpersonal
relationships

Diana Dwyer

First published 2000
by Routledge
11 New Fetter Lane, London EC4P 4EE

Simultaneously published in the USA and Canada
by Taylor & Francis Inc.
325 Chestnut Street, Philadelphia PA 19106

Routledge is an imprint of the Taylor & Francis Group

© 2000 Diana Dwyer

Typeset in Times and Frutiger by Keystroke,
Jacaranda Lodge, Wolverhampton
Printed and bound in Great Britain by
TJ International Ltd, Padstow, Cornwall

British Library Cataloguing in Publication Data
A catalogue record for this book is available from the British Library

Library of Congress Cataloging in Publication Data
Dwyer, Diana, 1949–
Interpersonal relationships / Diana Dwyer.
p. cm. — (Routledge modular psychology)
Includes bibliographical references and index.
1. Interpersonal relations. I. Title. II. Series.
HM1106.D89 2000
158.2—dc21 99–38469
CIP

ISBN 0–415–19623–X (hbk)
ISBN 0–415–19624–8 (pbk)

This book is dedicated to two people with each of whom I have had a wonderful relationship – to my father, Doug Ginger, and to my late son Tony Dwyer – with deepest love.

Contents

Illustrations

Figures

Tables

Acknowledgements

The series editors and Routledge acknowledge the expert help of Paul Humphreys, Examiner and Reviser for A-level Psychology, in compiling the Study Aids section of each book in the series.

They also acknowledge the Association Examining Board (AEB) for granting permission to use their examination material. The AEB do not accept responsibility for the answers or examiner comment in the Study Aids section of this book or any other book in the series.

The author would also like to express her sincerest thanks to her father, Doug Ginger, for his help in reading the manuscript and offering encouragement and support as he has done throughout her life. Thanks dad!

1

Types of relationships

Introduction

Humans are essentially social beings. As countless novels, films, songs, plays and poems testify, our ultimate happiness and despair is founded in relationships. Satisfaction at work, at play and in family life depends largely on the quality of our friendships and loves. In a national survey, Campbell *et al.* (1976) found that most people consider it more important to have good friends and a happy family life than to have financial security. When Klinger (1977) posed the question 'What is it that makes your life meaningful?', almost all respondents mentioned being loved and wanted.

Research on interpersonal relationships

When studying interpersonal relationships, we are interested in trying to answer a great variety of questions. Why do we like some people and not others? What happens when we fall in love? What factors contribute to a successful marriage? What *is* a 'successful' marriage? How often do relatives keep in touch with each other? Can a relationship have an affect on your health? If so, how?

The list of questions is virtually endless, and this is one reason among many why no single method will suffice to provide all the answers. As with most aspects of social psychology, a variety of methods of research need to be employed when investigating interpersonal relationships, all of which have some advantages and some limitations. Answers will not come from a few studies; rather, our understanding of this area depends on the gradual accumulation of knowledge gleaned by many researchers looking at the same aspects of relationships in different ways. Let us now look at some of these methods.

Correlations

The method of **correlation** looks at whether there is an association between two variables. For example, we can measure the amount of attitude similarity between pairs of friends and the degree of satisfaction with the friendship (so, in this case, the variables are degree of attitude similarity and degree of relationship satisfaction). If we find that greater attitude similarity is associated with greater relationship satisfaction, there is a *positive correlation* between the two variables. This tells us that the more similar people are in their attitudes, the more satisfying they find the relationship. This is a useful piece of information in itself and can also be used as the basis for further investigations. However, correlational designs have a major disadvantage because they cannot tell us whether or not one variable *causes* another, and we are left with several unanswered questions about the reasons for the association. Do people choose friends because they have similar attitudes to themselves? This implies that attitude similarity *causes* friendship satisfaction. Alternatively, are people first attracted to someone and then, the more they like someone, the more they change their attitudes to match theirs? In this case, the implication is that friendship satisfaction *causes* attitude similarity. Yet another possibility is that people make friends with those from similar backgrounds because they are the people they meet in the course of their everyday lives, and people from similar backgrounds tend both to like each other and share similar attitudes. Unlike the first two possibilities, this one implies no direct cause and effect between the two variables but a third factor (similar background) that influences both of the other two.

Unfortunately, many people misinterpret the findings of correlational studies and jump to conclusions about cause and effect. Bear this in mind when you consider the research studies discussed in this text.

Experiments

The experimental method is the research tool that is ideally suited to establishing cause and effect. For example, we could ask people to complete a questionnaire about their own attitudes and then present them with various profiles of strangers and ask them to rate how positively they feel towards these people, based on the attitudes in the profile. The personal profiles can be varied by the experimenter on a scale ranging from very similar to very different attitudes from those of the participant. In this case, unlike the correlational design, we are manipulating one variable, called the **independent variable** (in this case, the extent of attitude similarity) while seeing what effect, if any, it has on the **dependent variable** (in this case, the degree of liking).

The major advantage of the experimental method is that it allows us to establish cause and effect. In our example we can see if attitude similarity *causes* liking. There are, however, many limitations to this design, especially with regard to research in interpersonal relationships. We cannot truly mimic how people relate to each other in real life. For example, everyday experiences of meeting someone new do not usually involve seeing a profile of them first and then consciously rating how we feel about them. Laboratory situations can never truly reflect the important factors in intimate relationships. For practical reasons we cannot, and for ethical reasons we should not, create love, jealousy and passion in the laboratory. With regard to interpersonal relationships, laboratory experiments are limited in that they can only really investigate fairly detached, emotionless interactions between strangers.

In essence then, correlational and experimental designs each have very different advantages and the two methods complement each other. Correlations allow us to look at real-life variables, such as love, sexual behaviour and commitment. This means that this method is likely to have **ecological validity**, that is, it can sample behaviour which exists in real life situations. However, it does not allow us to draw conclusions about cause and effect. The experimental design, in contrast, does allow us to establish causal factors but we can only study a very narrow range of behaviour associated with relationships, so this method is likely to lack ecological validity. This is precisely why we need to use more than one method.

Selection of participants

Another problem with which researchers in interpersonal relationships are faced is the selection of participants to take part in investigations. In an ideal world, we would look in detail at a large and representative sample of the population, drawn from all sorts of walks of life – people of all ages, from a wide variety of cultural and socioeconomic backgrounds. Unfortunately, obtaining such a sample is difficult and expensive. In addition to this, when investigating a very large number of people, it is difficult to obtain really detailed information from them. If, for example, a wide-scale survey were to be conducted, only a limited amount of information could be obtained from each participant. It is only feasible to obtain in-depth information from a relatively small number of participants.

As you will see as you read this book, a commonly used sampling method employed by researchers is to draw on those people who are readily available, such as students. Such an **opportunity sample** (or convenience sample) means that invariably the sample consists of a very narrow range of participants in terms of age, educational and socioeconomic status and cultural background. What we must bear in mind is that, in any psychological investigation, the results obtained only apply to people who have the same characteristics as the participants. Studies conducted on students cannot be generalised to the broader population.

The development of research in interpersonal relationships

It is reasonable to say that, until fairly recently, the research into interpersonal relationships was very restricted but it has changed considerably since these early, very limited beginnings. Duck (1995) has pointed out how inadequate and artificial were the early studies in this area which concentrated mainly on first impressions and the factors involved in what made one person attractive to another. The methods used were mainly laboratory studies in which samples of college students were asked for their almost immediate reactions to strangers, or responses to a bogus person who had completed an attitude questionnaire. In the latter case, absolutely no contact between real-life people ever took place. Alternatively, hapless students were paired in huge 'blind date' arrangements and information gleaned on how they rated their 'date' and whether they would choose to see them again (e.g. Walster *et al.*, 1966). The limited information obtained was then used to formulate far-reaching theories about the basis of friendship or of relationship satisfaction. Duck (1995) complained that such research did not look at many of the run-of-the-mill interactions involved in everyday life, such as playfulness and joking, managing routines like cooking, cleaning and bathing the children, and the mutual understanding that derives from such ordinary interchange.

Nowadays, research into interpersonal relationships is far broader and presents a much more complex picture of human relationships. It includes not only the positive elements – the delights, laughter and joy of friendship, romance and family – but also the negative elements – the irritations and annoyances that we all recognise as part and parcel of relationships. It also tends to look at the course of real-life relationships over a considerable period of time and thereby investigates the factors that contribute to satisfaction, dissatisfaction and the means by which we deal with the changes in our feelings towards other people. Such research has a wide variety of practical applications and contributes greatly to our understanding of what makes us happy and what makes us profoundly miserable.

As with many areas of psychology, much of the research on relationships is limited to very few cultures. Moghaddam *et al.* (1993) point out that most research in this area has largely ignored those that are important in Eastern 'collectivist' societies and has been concerned almost exclusively with relationships that are important in Western, 'individualistic' cultures – those of initial attraction, friendship choices and mate selection. These relationships are those which are most important in the mobile, urban, Western world in which new acquaintances are made on an almost daily basis, the media flaunts sex and passion and the selection of a heterosexual partner is based on a belief in romantic love. The focus is very much on choice and on the buildup and breakdown of relationships which are regarded as temporary. In contrast, little attention has been paid to such relationships as kinship and community, the relatively permanent, compulsory relationships which are central to many Eastern, collectivist cultures in which group goals rather than personal goals are paramount. (These ideas are discussed in detail in Chapter 8.) Although some recent research, especially in Britain (e.g. Argyle and Henderson, 1986), has taken a cross-cultural approach and looked at both kinship and the norms and rules of relationships in a variety of cultures, the research has a long way to go before we can formulate any universal theories concerning all types of interpersonal and intergroup relationships.

Progress exercise

1 When researching interpersonal relationships, why are correlational methods likely to have greater ecological validity than experimental methods?
2 What is the main advantage of using experiments to investigate interpersonal relationships?
3 What are the problems associated with trying to obtain a representative sample of participants when researching interpersonal relationships?
4 What is the limitation of using an opportunity sample comprising university students?

Types of relationships

We experience a large number of relationships in our lives. For many of us, the first important ones will be those with our parents and other close relatives. As we grow up, other relationships become important: we make friends, we go to work, we have romantic liaisons – all of these everyday life events involve interpersonal interactions which greatly influence the quality of our lives. We will start by considering **affiliation**, our basic need to associate with others and then turn our attention to some specific relationships that are likely to be of significance to us.

Affiliation

Affiliation is the basic need for the company of others. One of the most devastating punishments we can inflict on humans is to place them in solitary confinement, thereby forcing them to be completely alone. Across most societies and situations, humans show gregarious (sociable) tendencies, indicating that the need to affiliate is at least in part instinctive. We live and work in groups rather than in isolation; indeed, our very survival depends on it. We affiliate in all manner of circumstances such as to have fun, to gain approval, to alleviate fear and to share sexual intimacies.

The motivation to be with others comes from both the inside and the outside in that it depends on both personality and circumstances. Certain situations that we face, especially new, frightening or ambiguous ones, lead us to seek out others. However, people also differ in their need for affiliation, some being far more sociable than others.

Situational factors in affiliation

Think about the occasions when you most want to be with others and those when you yearn for solitude. A survey conducted by Fox (1980) showed that people are particularly keen to be with others under *pleasant* conditions and under *threatening* ones. If we want to enjoy ourselves – for example, visit a pub, watch a football match, go to the cinema – most of us prefer to be with others rather than alone and our triumphs feel better when shared ('I'm bursting to tell you – I've just passed my driving test'). When we feel *alarmed* or *frightened* we also seek out company ('I'm not going into that house alone, my Aunt Nelly swears it's haunted').

Fox's survey indicated that we prefer to be alone under certain *unpleasant* circumstances, such as when we are nervous and tense before an important interview or have just failed a test, and under conditions that *require concentration*, such as when we have a difficult exam for which we need to revise.

Unfortunately, research on affiliation has tended to concentrate mainly on artificial situations, usually stressful ones, in which the desire or otherwise to be with another person can be easily measured. A typical example is an early, often referenced study by Schachter (1959). He induced high levels of anxiety in the experimental group of participants by leading them to expect severe, painful electric shocks during the procedure to follow. Control participants who were in the low-anxiety condition were led to expect extremely mild shocks that would merely tingle. All participants were then asked if they would prefer to wait alone or with others. Sixty-three per cent of those in the high-anxiety condition, as opposed to only 33 per cent in the low-anxiety condition, chose to wait in the company of others, indicating that *anxiety increases the need to affiliate*. In later studies it was shown that, given a choice, fearful individuals chose to associate with people in the same boat (also expecting severe shocks) rather than with those who had nothing to fear. In a now classic quote, Schachter remarked that 'Misery doesn't love just any kind of company; it loves only miserable company' (Schachter, 1959, p. 24).

It should be noted that Schachter's study was ethically questionable since the anticipation of a severe shock almost certainly made people feel fearful and tense. It was also conducted under very artificial conditions and could therefore be said to lack ecological validity.

One study conducted in a more real-life situation indicated that people in stressful circumstances do not always choose to be with those expecting a similar fate. Kulik and Mahler (1989) found that cancer patients who were about to undergo an operation preferred being with people who had successfully recovered from such an operation rather than with people in a similar situation to their own. This highlights the fact that when we are facing an unknown threat, we turn to people who have greater experience in the hope that they can allay our fears or at least provide information.

Motives for affiliation

Buunk (1996) suggests that there are many motives that drive people to affiliate, but that the three main ones are: social comparison, anxiety reduction and information seeking.

- *Social comparison* In a refreshingly naturalistic study, Buunk and VanYperen (1991) found that people who are uncertain about their marriage, especially if they are unhappy with it, like to discuss this with people in a similar situation, i.e. to make social comparisons. **Social comparison theory**, formulated by Festinger (1954), states that people want to compare their own feelings and reactions with those of others in the same situation. This is especially true when we are in a new or fearful situation.

- *Anxiety reduction* We have already seen that in fearful circumstances, given the choice, we prefer to be with people who have already encountered the situation rather than people who are about to have the same experience (e.g. Kulik and Mahler, 1989). In these conditions then, social comparison gives way to an attempt to reduce anxiety by turning to sympathetic people who might offer emotional support and reassurance.
- *Information seeking* Studies like that of Kulik and Mahler (1989), mentioned above, also indicate that in fearful circumstances adults, like children, seek reassurance from those who are more knowledgeable than themselves; and who better than those who have experienced the same danger?

These three motives are not, of course, mutually exclusive. In many circumstances all three may be operating. In a real-life situation we are not forced to choose between one group of people and another and we may, especially when frightened, affiliate with a variety of people who together satisfy all three motives. For example, someone who is newly diagnosed as having bowel cancer is likely to seek out experts and former sufferers who can provide information and, hopefully, reduce anxiety. He or she is also likely to talk to others who have been newly diagnosed, and with whom it is possible to empathise and sympathise and from whom social comparison information can be obtained. Last but not least, he or she will turn to close friends and family for emotional support during this difficult time.

Personality factors in affiliation

Even though there are situations in which we are more likely to seek the company of others, some people will always be more inclined to socialise than others. There are essential differences in the characteristics and behaviour of people who have a high need to affiliate as opposed to those who are low in this need. In general, people who are high in the need to affiliate are concerned about establishing and maintaining positive relationships with others and tend to watch other people closely in social interactions. They are friendly towards others and tend to be popular. Perhaps because they are concerned to be accepted by others they are fearful of rejection, are careful not to offend others and show high levels of anxiety in social settings. Essentially, then, although the need to affiliate is a basic one, this need is greater for some people than for others.

1 Under what circumstances do we particularly like to be with others and when do we prefer to be alone?
2 Look back over the last two weeks and try to think of circumstances in which you would have preferred to be alone, and/or those when you wanted to be with other people. Do they correspond to the situations outlined in the answer to question 1?
3 The study by Kulik and Mahler (1989) could be described as having more ecological validity than the study by Schachter (1959). What is ecological validity? (If in doubt, look in the glossary.) Why could these two studies be said to differ in this respect? (Remember to include this in the *evaluation* of the studies.)

Friendship

Friends are people we like and with whom we enjoy doing things. The well-known saying, 'you can choose your friends but you cannot choose your family', reflects the fact that, unlike kinship, friendship is entirely voluntary. Friendship is universal: at all ages, in all classes and cultures, men and women, boys and girls, form bonds of friendship.

Argyle and Henderson (1985) outlined the norms and rules that are most important in friendship (see Chapter 7). Friends freely help in times of need; they trust and respect each other and share confidences while respecting each other's privacy. They do not criticise each other in public and will not tolerate others being unpleasant about friends who are not there to defend themselves.

There is considerable variation in the degree of intimacy and the stability of friendships. Childhood friendships tend to be fairly unstable, while those made during adolescence and early adulthood are often the closest and most enduring.

Changes in friendship with age

Until recently, psychologists have paid little attention to peer relationships in childhood, concentrating instead on parent–child relationships. Now the focus is changing. It has become clear that peer relationships play a significant and unique role in children's development, helping them in the transition from the dependence of childhood to the independence of young adulthood.

Friendships take different forms and serve different purposes at various stages of life. Although preschool children show more intimate behaviour with some peers than with others, at this age they have no concept of friendship as an enduring kind of relationship: friends are essentially playmates.

From about the age of 8, children begin to see friends as people who can be trusted to be loyal, kind, cooperative and sensitive to the other's needs (Pataki *et al.*, 1994). In adolescence there is an emphasis on friends being people who truly understand each other's strengths and weaknesses and are willing to confide their innermost feelings (Hartup, 1992). During adolescence, same-sex friendships are probably more intense than at any other age.

As people grow older and marry, friendship becomes less central to their lives and not as close. Adults tend to draw their friends from the immediate neighbourhood and from work; these relationships are usually less intimate than those based on early attachments (Argyle and Henderson, 1985).

Contrary to popular belief, most older people (those above the age of 60) are not lonely and friendless; the vast majority have at least one close friend. Friends in late adulthood provide intimacy, people with whom to share activities, and are a source of excitement and joy (Adams, 1986). Friends are especially important to elderly women who are more likely to be widowed than men.

From an early age and throughout life, males and females show significant differences in styles of friendship. These are discussed in Chapter 8.

Relationships with relations

For the vast majority of people, relationships with our family members, especially with our parents and children, are a vital feature of our social network from the cradle to the grave. However much they may at times cause intense irritation, our families serve a vital function in our lives, providing us with a shared identity and a safe base.

Despite the popular stereotype of the isolated nuclear family in the Western world, links between family members in different geographical households are often very close – especially in these days of telephones, faxes and e-mails. Finch and Mason (1993) found that the majority of adults have some contact with their mothers at least once a week and over 10 per cent see them daily. No matter how great the distance between parents and children, links remain strong, the strongest typically being with mothers. There is a sense of obligation to remain in touch with all immediate family members, but especially with parents. However, this sense of obligation does not detract from the fact that links are also maintained through mutual enjoyment – we do not only keep in touch because we 'have to' but because we want to.

Sibling relationships are often the most enduring of all relationships in our lives and are exceptional for the sheer amount of shared experience. Although the intensity of sibling relationships varies enormously, most people report feeling close to their brothers and sisters at least in some respects (Bank, 1992). Relationships between sisters are by far the strongest, but all of them provide a great deal of emotional support and warmth despite the fact that there may also be some rivalry.

Often the closest relationship with relatives outside the immediate family is that between grandparents and grandchildren. Grandparents are quite close to their grandchildren because they have little disciplinary responsibility and can simply enjoy the company of the young. From the grandchild's perspective, grandparents are people with whom you can have fun and to whom you can sometimes turn when you are in mum and dad's bad books.

Romantic relationships

According to Hatfield and Rapson (1987), the earliest stages of a passionate relationship involve quite spectacular and specific cognitive, behavioural and emotional aspects. When we 'fall in love' we are at first totally preoccupied with the object of our passion and have a great desire to get to know them and be known to them. Emotions run high and may be positive or negative. If everything is going well, we are likely to be on top of the world but be plunged into the depths of despair if our love is not reciprocated. Either way, there is a high level of physiological arousal and a certain degree of uncertainty and anxiety. We have a fascination with the object of our love, a great sexual desire for them and feel the need to cherish and care for them. In the early stages, lovers whose passion is mutual want to spend as much time as possible together, often becoming absorbed in each other to the exclusion of everyone else.

Walster and Walster (1978) claim, as have many others, that passionate love is extremely fragile and unenduring, in contrast to other types of love which may last a lifetime. Many studies have indeed shown that romantic love fades over time, sometimes, but certainly not always, to be replaced by companionate love. Since love is the topic area of Chapter 2, we will at this stage elaborate no further on romantic relationships.

1 Make a list of the advantages and disadvantages of both the correlational method and the experimental method when investigating interpersonal relationships.
2 What criticisms of research on interpersonal relationships are mentioned by Duck (1995)?
3 What limitations are discussed by Moghaddam *et al.* (1993)?
4 Compared to the amount of research concentrated on romantic relationships, there is comparatively little on kinship ties. What reasons would Moghaddam *et al.* give for this difference in research interests among Western psychologists?

Review exercise

Summary

• No single research method is adequate to study interpersonal relationships. Correlational designs can have fairly high ecological validity but do not allow us to establish cause and effect relationships. Experiments can establish cause and effect but measure very limited factors in artificial surroundings.
• Early research on interpersonal relationships has been criticised

for being artificial in its research design and limited in its scope. Firstly, it has tended to concentrate on initial impressions under laboratory conditions. Secondly, most research in this area has been concerned almost exclusively with relationships that are important in Western, 'individualistic' cultures rather than those that are central to the Eastern, 'collectivist' societies.

- Affiliation is the basic need for the company of others. It is especially strong under both pleasant and threatening conditions. According to Buunk (1996), the three main reasons why people want be with others are social comparison, anxiety reduction and information seeking.
- Friendship is a voluntary relationship with people whom we like. Friends help in times of need, trust and respect each other, and share confidences while respecting each other's privacy. Friendship is important throughout life but particularly in adolescence.
- Relationships with family members are the most enduring of all relationships. Most adults are in touch with their mothers at least once a week. Families serve a vital function, providing a sense of identity and a secure base.

Further reading

Argyle, M. and Henderson, M. (1985) *The Anatomy of Relationships*, Harmondsworth: Penguin. Chapter 4 looks in detail at friendship and Chapter 9 at kinship. Other relationships considered are those with neighbours and work colleagues. It also discusses many topic areas covered later in this book, such as relationship rules. This book is easy to read and detailed in research. It covers many areas that other books don't reach.

Cramer, D. (1998) *Close Relationships*, London: Edward Arnold. Chapter 1 covers the basics in researching interpersonal relationships, detailing the problems, limitations and uses of each type of research method.

2

Types of love

- The basic distinction: companionate and passionate love
- Rubin's model of liking and loving
- Sternberg's triangle of love
- Lee's six styles of loving
- Types of love and attachment styles

Although we use the expression 'love' to describe our feelings towards our closest friends, our parents and our romantic partners, we know that the emotions we feel in each case are by no means identical. We also appreciate that when we talk of *liking* one particular friend and *loving* another, the feelings we have for each of them may not be so very different. They vary in quantity rather than in quality. In this chapter, we will look at the ways in which social psychologists have classified different types of love.

The basic distinction: companionate and passionate love

Berscheid and Walster (1978) distinguish between *liking*, *companionate love* and *passionate (romantic) love*. Liking and companionate love are considered to be extremes on a continuum, the only difference being the depth of feeling and the degree of involvement. Passionate love, on the other hand, is quite a different matter.

- *Liking* is the affection we feel for casual acquaintances.
- *Companionate love* is the affection we feel for those with whom our lives are deeply entwined.
- *Passionate love* is a powerful emotional state that involves overwhelming feelings of tenderness, elation, anxiety and sexual desire.

Berscheid *et al.* (1989) and Hatfield and Walster (1978) suggest that the important differences between companionate and passionate love are:

- Companionate love (and liking) develops through mutual actual rewards while passionate love is based on imagined gratification and fantasy.
- Passionate love becomes diluted over time whereas companionate love tends to deepen and intensify.
- Passionate love thrives on novelty and uncertainty while companionate love is founded on familiarity and predictability.
- Companionate love is a totally positive emotion, whereas the emotions involved in passionate love are both positive and negative. When we fall in love, we experience joy and excitement, jealousy and anxiety.

Rubin's model of liking and loving

In order to explore the concepts of liking and different types of loving, it is necessary to have some means of measuring them. Rubin (1970, 1973), one of the first social psychologists to attempt to measure liking and love, devised both a Love scale and a Liking scale. The research carried out to compile these scales also led Rubin to draw a distinction between liking and the type of loving as expressed by dating couples. Liking was concerned with affection and respect. Loving, according to Rubin, consisted of three components:

- *Attachment* A strong need for the physical presence and support of the loved one and the desire to be fulfilled by them.
- *Caring* A feeling of concern for the loved one manifested in the desire to help and support them.
- *Intimacy* A desire for close and confidential contact with the loved one in an atmosphere of trust.

Rubin asked dating couples to complete both the Liking and Loving scales as applied to their dating partner and to a close friend. Here are some items from both scales: the first three are from the Liking scale and the last three from the Loving scale. For each item, the answer is on a scale from 1 = not at all to 10 = totally.

1 This person is one of the most likeable people I know.
2 This person is the sort of person I would like to be.
3 I have great confidence in this person's good judgements.
4 I feel I can confide in this person about virtually anything.
5 I would forgive this person for practically anything.
6 I would do almost anything for this person.

(Based on Rubin, 1973)

Rubin found that with regard to how the couples felt about each other there was not much difference between the men and women in the love they expressed, but the women tended to like the men more than the men liked the women. Men and women rated liking for same-sex friends equally, but women tended to express more love for their friends. It has been suggested that with regard to adult relationships, men tend to love only within the context of a sexual relationship whereas women are more likely to experience at least some of the components of attachment, caring and, to a lesser extent, intimacy with a wide variety of people.

Commentary

Although some have argued that it is impossible to measure love, results show that the scales devised by Rubin do have some validity. In experimental sessions, Rubin (1973) found that couples who scored high on the Love scale made more eye contact and were more likely to say they were in love. In a six-month follow-up study, scores on the Rubin Love scale successfully predicted how successful a relationship was. People who scored high on the Love scale were more likely to be still together and to have committed themselves to a permanent relationship.

We will now turn to other ways in which types of love have been classified. You will notice that though these classifications are more complex than that of the simple differentiation between passionate and companionate love, they all use this as a basic distinction.

Sternberg's triangle of love

Sternberg sees love as having three central components:

- *Intimacy* – the *emotional* component. This involves sharing, mutual understanding and emotional support. It creates warmth in a relationship.
- *Passion* – the *motivational* component. This involves physical attraction, sexual desire and the feeling of being 'in love'. Although sexual needs are very important in passion, other needs may also be involved, such as the need for self-esteem and affiliation.
- *Commitment/decision* – the *cognitive* component. This involves a short-term decision that you love someone and a longer-term commitment to maintain that love.

These components of love can be combined in different ways to produce seven varieties of love, as shown in Table 1, pp.20–21.

Progress exercise

Think of some films, books and plays that are based on the theme of romantic love. You could include *Ghost*, *Titanic*, *My Best Friend's Wedding*, *There's Something about Mary*. Consider which of Sternberg's types of love are the main theme in each of these works.

Sternberg argues that it is essential to recognise that each of the three components – intimacy, passion and commitment/decision – differs in how long it lasts and the speed with which it fades. Passion rises quickly and then typically fades fast; commitment gradually rises and then levels off; intimacy grows slowly and steadily over a period of time. Part of the success, or otherwise, of relationships depends on our ability to change as each of the components changes.

Commentary

Sternberg's theory, unlike most of its predecessors, offers more than one or two kinds of love. It therefore helps us to see love as a multiple rather than a unitary phenomenon.

It also has certain practical applications. Firstly, by measuring the three components, it is possible to get a sense of where each partner in a loving relationship stands. Secondly, by analysing differences between the types of love shown by both members of a couple, it helps pinpoint areas where change and compromise may be necessary if the relationship is to endure.

One problem with the model is that the decision/commitment component is not clearly defined, and it is therefore difficult to ascertain on what basis an individual decides to love another person (Cramer, 1998).

Lee's six styles of loving

Based on survey material of adults in the US, Canada and Great Britain, Lee (1973), a sociologist, suggests that there are six styles of loving (Table 2).

Commentary

These love styles can be seen in terms of Sternberg's components. Romantic love (eros), for example, has large amounts of passion while companionate love (storge) has high degrees of commitment and intimacy but little passion.

Hendrick and Hendrick (1989) developed a 'love questionnaire' to empirically investigate these love styles. They found that there was evidence to support the idea of distinct love styles. However, individuals could rarely be classified into only one type: each individual may show a combination of styles.

One difference in such love styles is based on gender. Hendrick *et al.* (1984) found that men were more likely to believe in love at first sight (romantic love) and to be game-players. Women were more likely to be pragmatic in their choice of partner or to experience companionate love.

Cramer (1987) administered a questionnaire based on Lee's styles of loving to a group of undergraduates. He suggests that the items

Table 1 Sternberg's type of love and their components

Component			Type of love	Example
Intimacy	Passion	Commitment/decision		
✓	—	—	Liking	The feeling involved in true and deep friendships. There is closeness and warmth but no passion or long-term commitment
—	✓	—	Infatuation	Obsession with an idealised partner rather than a real person, typical of 'love at first sight'. It involves a high degree of physical and mental arousal and tends to last only if the relationship is not consummated.
—	—	✓	Empty love	Typical of the kind of love in a long-term stagnant relationship in which people have lost mutual emotional involvement and stay together due to habit, fear of change or 'for the sake of the children'.

Component			Type of love	Example
Intimacy	Passion	Commitment/decision		
✓	✓	—	Romantic love	Love based on both physical and emotional attraction. Typical of the love between Romeo and Juliet in which the lovers feel mutual passion accompanied by the feeling that they can bare their souls to one another.
✓	—	✓	Companionate love	The love that exists in a long-term committed friendship or in a marriage in which physical attraction has waned. Most romantic love relationships that last eventually turn into companionate love relationships.
—	✓	✓	Fatuous love	Commitment made on the basis of passion alone as typified by a 'whirlwind romance'. Because intimacy has had no time to develop, and passion soon fades, partners feel short-changed and disappointed and the relationship is likely to be very short-lived.
✓	✓	✓	Consummate love	A complete love towards which many people strive, especially in romantic relationships. We do not seek this kind of love in many of our relationships, just those that mean the most to us.

Table 2 Lee's six styles of loving		
Type of love	*Greek name*	*Description*
Romantic love	Eros	An all-consuming emotional experience, an immediate powerful physical attraction to someone.
Companionate love	Storge	A comfortable intimacy that grows slowly and involves mutual sharing and gradual self-disclosure.
Game-playing love	Ludus	Love based on fun and strategy with no commitment and a belief in 'playing the field'. It is usually short-lived and will end as soon as boredom sets in.
Possessive love	Mania	An emotionally intense, jealous, obsessive love shown by an anxious individual who lives in constant fear of rejection.
Pragmatic love	Pragma	A logical love based on selecting a partner who satisfies practical needs and is a match in terms of age, religion, background and personality. There is contentment rather than excitement.
Altruistic love	Agape	An unconditional, caring, giving and forgiving type of love. There is no expectation of reciprocity; love is self-sacrificing.

can be meaningfully grouped into four categories: relationship satisfaction, relationship openness, relationship importance and physical intimacy. The scores on these four factors correlated with five of the love styles – those of romantic love (eros), possessive love (mania), companionate love (storge), pragmatic love (pragma) and game-playing love (ludus). For example, physical intimacy was positively correlated with eros but negatively correlated with storge. The factors of relationship satisfaction, relationship openness, relationship importance and physical intimacy could therefore be used to differentiate the love styles.

The theories of Lee and Sternberg are largely descriptive; they tell us which styles people use but say little about why these styles have been adopted. The next theory attempts to do just this by drawing parallels between childhood experiences and later adult relationships.

Types of love and attachment styles

Hazan and Shaver (1987, 1990) argue that the kinds of attachment bonds we form in childhood influence the style of loving we experience as an adult. Ainsworth *et al.* (1978) proposed that, as a consequence of the way in which adults were treated as babies, infants show three **attachment styles** towards their parents: *secure, avoidant or ambivalent (anxious/insecure)* (see Flanagan, 1999 for a broader discussion of these attachment styles). According to Hazan and Shaver, each of these forms of attachment is related to later loving in the following ways.

- Those who showed *secure attachment* in infancy are confident in their adult relationships, find it easy to get close to people and are not unduly worried about being rejected. They are quite happy to be dependent and have people depend on them; they are trusting and stable.
- Those who were *avoidant* in infancy tend to become nervous when people get too close to them and are unwilling to depend on others. They fear that a potential partner may expect to become more intimate than they themselves would like. They are detached and unresponsive.
- Those who showed *ambivalent (anxious or insecure) attachment* in early childhood worry that their partners do not really love them, at least with the intensity they would like. These people would like to merge completely with their partner. They are anxious and uncertain.

Hazan and Shaver (1987) asked adults to select from three descriptions the one that most closely resembled the way they felt. The choices they were given were as follows:

A I find it relatively easy to get close to others and am comfortable depending on them and having them depend on me. I don't often worry about being abandoned or about someone getting too close to me.

B I am somewhat uncomfortable being close to others. I find it difficult to trust them completely, difficult to allow myself to depend on them. I am nervous when anyone gets too close, and love partners often want me to be more intimate than I feel comfortable being.

C I find that others are reluctant to get as close as I would like. I often worry that my partner doesn't really love me or won't want to stay with me. I want to merge completely with another person, and this desire sometimes scares people away.

A = secure   B = avoidant   C = anxious/ambivalent

(From Shaver *et al.*, 1988)

The respondents also answered a variety of specific questions about their experiences in romantic relationships. In general, adults with secure attachment styles found happiness, trust and friendship in their relationships. Those with the avoidant style showed a fear of intimacy and a reluctance to commit at all. Individuals with an anxious style reported experiencing extremes of emotions, including a desire for love at first sight and obsessive preoccupations with regard to the object of their desire.

In support of their theory, Hazan and Shaver point out that the percentage of the three styles of attachment found in adults approximates very closely to that found in infants: 60 per cent are secure, 20 to 25 per cent are avoidant and 15 to 20 per cent are ambivalent. Furthermore, adults with different attachment styles reported different childhood experiences which were broadly in line with what the theory would predict. Secure individuals reported positive family relationships; avoidant individuals spoke of difficulties with their mother and ambivalent people mentioned difficulties with their father (Hazan and Shaver, 1987).

Commentary

Hazan and Shaver argue that adult attachments, like infant ones, serve a biological purpose. Just as infant–caregiver attachment serves the survival function of keeping the baby near the adult because separation could result in death, so adult attachments are designed by evolution to bind together potential parents so that the infant will have reliable care.

How enduring are these attachment styles? Kirkpatrick and Hazan (1994) reported that 70 per cent of respondents chose the same attachment style as they had four years previously. This shows that in the majority of cases attachment style remained stable, but we must not lose sight of the fact that nearly one-third of individuals did show a change.

It is recognised that infant attachment styles are not the only influence on later relationships. Hazan herself pointed out that changes in attachment styles may be related to experience in later romantic relationships (Hazan *et al.*, 1991). These researchers found that secure individuals who had experienced a disastrous relationship in adulthood were more likely to become insecure, whereas a successful romance may make individuals more secure.

Levitt (1991) argues that it is too simple to view the quality of later relationships being dependent solely on the initial parent–child attachment. People bring all sorts of expectations to a relationship (as pointed out by e.g. Argyle *et al.*, 1985; Duck, 1988) and have many experiences that are influential. Levitt believes that infant attachments almost certainly have an influence, but so do other factors, such as our general understanding of people, our cultural norms (such as our shared beliefs about how lovers should behave) and our personal ideologies (such as feminism or traditionalist).

In essence then, attachment styles in adult life may depend both on what we bring to a relationship and what we get from it.

In this chapter we have looked at a variety of ways in which social psychologists have classified that all-important emotion of love, but just how successful have they been in answering the question 'What is love?' It does appear that the contrast between passionate and companionate love may well be the most important distinction, but attempts to integrate the models further have not been very successful. As Brehm (1992) comments: 'Like Shakespeare, social scientists have discovered that attempting to answer the question "What is love?" is by no means an easy task' (p. 110).

1   The table below lists the seven types of loving detailed in Sternberg's theory. Place ticks in the relevant boxes to correspond to the presence of each of the three components: intimacy, passion, commitment/decision. Try to do it initially from commonsense expectation, then check your answers with table 1.

Type of love	Intimacy	Passion	Commitment
Liking			
Infatuation			
Empty love			
Romantic love			
Companionate love			
Fatuous love			
Consummate love			

2   Devise a brief story to illustrate any three of Lee's styles of loving. If it is feasible, swap with a fellow student who has done the same exercise and ask him or her to ascertain which love styles you are describing and vice versa.

3   Evaluate Hazan and Shaver's theory of attachment styles (you could do this by listing the evidence in support of it and then considering its limitations).

Summary

- Liking, loving and falling in love are distinct one from the other. Liking is affection we feel for casual acquaintances. Companionate love is the deeper affection we feel for those with whom our lives are deeply entwined. Passionate love is a powerful emotional state that involves strong feelings of elation and sexual desire together with some anxiety.

- Rubin developed scales to measure loving and liking. He believed that love had three components: attachment, caring and intimacy.

- Sternberg sees love as having three central components: intimacy, passion and commitment. These can be combined in different ways to produce seven varieties of love.
- Lee suggests that there are six styles of loving: romantic, companionate, game-playing, possessive, pragmatic and altruistic.
- Hazan and Shaver suggest that the styles of loving we show in adulthood reflect the attachment bonds we formed in early child-hood: secure, anxious or avoidant.

Further reading

Brehm, S.S. (1992) *Intimate Relationships*, New York: McGraw-Hill. Chapter 4, 'Love and romance', gives an overview of theories of types of love with examples of items from questionnaires and scales used to measure love. The chapter starts with a brief and fascinating history of love.

Sternberg, R.J. and Barnes, M. L. (eds) (1988) *The Psychology of Love*, New Haven and London: Yale University Press. This book is invaluable as it contains papers on all the important theories. Chapter 6 gives a detailed account by Sternberg of his triangular theory with an appropriate tale to illustrate each type of love (. . . Tim and Diana met on a cruise to the Bahamas). Chapter 3 covers Lee's styles of love, and Chapter 4 gives an account of Hazan and Shaver's theory of attachment styles. There are plenty of other useful papers, including individual and cultural perspectives on romantic love.

3

Factors determining relationship formation

Proximity
Similarity
Physical attraction
Reciprocal liking
Complementarity
Competence

Think back to the circumstances in which you met your closest friends. Perhaps it was through school, college, work, or because they lived in the same street. At school and in other situations, such as work, there are many people with whom you could have made friends. Why did you make friends with certain people and not others? What factors attracted you to them and them to you?

In this chapter, we are going to look at research findings into the factors which help determine the onset of friendship or romance and the reasons why these factors may be influential.

Proximity

The single most important factor in predicting our likely choice of friends is the 'nearness' or *proximity* (also called *propinquity*) between you and them. Because of where we live, sit in a classroom or earn a living we have close contact with particular people, and it is this physical arrangement that is hugely influential in determining friendship patterns.

Festinger *et al.* (1950) observed the friendships that formed in a block of apartments for married students consisting of seventeen separate buildings, each comprising ten flats on two floors. More than ten times as many friendships formed between students who shared the same building than between students in different ones. Within the same building, friendships were far more likely between people who lived on the same floor than between those on different floors.

It was not only physical distance which made a difference. The most popular people were those who had apartments nearest the staircases and postboxes. This finding indicates that physical distance is not the only predictor of attraction. The **functional distance**, that is, the likelihood of two people coming into contact, is also very influential. In fact, as this study demonstrates, architectural features can significantly affect the likelihood that people will make friends. Those who live in apartments or rooms not often passed by others are liable to make far fewer friends than those who live near communal areas such as shared bathrooms, kitchens, lounges and stairways. People allocated rooms at the end of a corridor, away from the main thoroughfares, may initially welcome the privacy and peace this offers, but may eventually feel isolated and lonely. This also applies on housing estates. Those living at the end of a cul-de-sac are likely to have fewer friends in the immediate locality than those whose houses are situated on busy intersections.

Several other studies support the importance of both physical distance and functional distance in friendship formation. Segal (1974) monitored the friendship patterns of police cadets who were assigned to their rooms and to seats in classrooms according to the alphabetical order of their surname. He found that friendships tended to form between people whose surnames were close in the alphabet.

Yinin *et al.* (1977) compared friendships in Israeli dormitories that differed in the amount of interaction they permitted. In some dormitories students had their own *en-suite* facilities and had little cause to interact. In others, the toilets, showers and kitchens were all shared, resulting in high interaction. The higher the level of inter-action, the higher the proportion of friends chosen from within the living unit. Again, this demonstrates that it is functional distance rather than simply physical distance that influences the choice of friends: the more often people cross our path, the more likely we are to become friends with them.

This pattern does not just apply to youth. Nehamow and Lawton (1975) found that of the friendships between elderly people living in an urban housing complex, 88 per cent were formed by those living in the same building.

Neither does it apply simply to friendship: love tends to blossom at close quarters. Bossard (1932) examined the pre-marital addresses of the first 5,000 couples married in one city in 1931. More than half of the couples had lived within short walking distance of each other. Similar studies conducted around the same time in other cities confirm these findings. It might be interesting to repeat the studies to see whether, in a more mobile age, cohabiting couples still tend to originate from similar areas.

Perhaps one of the most important studies in this area is that by Deutsch and Collins (1951), who found that when people were assigned to rented public housing without regard to their race, many interracial friendships developed among the residents. This has obvious implications for racial harmony.

Exceptions

One of the problems of studies like that of Festinger *et al.* (1950) is that they are looking at a homogeneous (similar) group of people settling into a new situation. Everyone is of equal status and likely to cooperate. Under these conditions friendships are likely to form out of propinquity. On the other hand, proximity does not always lead to attraction, as anyone who has watched the television programme *Neighbours from Hell* can testify. Ebbesen *et al.* (1976) point out what many of us have experienced – that while the people we most like live only a short distance away, so do those we most intensely dislike. If your first experience of someone is negative, propinquity is likely to intensify this dislike. Fortunately for us, most first encounters are either neutral or positive, so we don't spend our lives surrounded by people we loathe.

A second limitation to the general rule is that when we encounter people too frequently we may become bored with them and tire of the relationship.

Why is proximity important?

There are several reasons why the physical or functional distance between two people will predict friendship.

1 *Familiarity*: many researchers believe that the reason we like those people whom we see most often is because they are familiar to us. Zajonc (1968) argues that *mere exposure* to someone is sufficient to make us like them, as has been demonstrated in several studies. For example, Moreland and Beach (1992) arranged for female confederates who were similar in appearance to attend either none, five, ten or fifteen seminar sessions. Using photos of the confederates, they then asked students from the seminars to assess how likeable they considered the females to be. The more often they had seen the confederate, the more highly they rated her.

2 *Exposure*: politicians are well aware of the effect of exposure and will attempt to have their 'mugshots' given maximum exposure before an election on the grounds that the more familiar their face and name, the more likely people are to vote for them.

3 *Low costs*: it takes little time or effort to interact with someone whom you meet on a regular basis and this gives you more opportunity to get to know them. The more you see someone, the more opportunity you have to discover mutual interests.

4 *Expectation of continued interaction*: when we expect to encounter people on a regular basis, and we cannot avoid them (at work, for instance), we try harder to see the good side of these people. We tend to exaggerate their positive points and minimise their negative ones. Given that they are likely to react in the same way, friendship becomes very probable.

5 *Predictability*: within reason, we prefer our environment to be predictable. When people are unpredictable we feel nervous, anxious and uncomfortable. When they are predicable we feel safe and relaxed. Note that I said *within reason* – if people are too predicable, they simply become boring.

6 *It makes evolutionary sense*: Burnstein *et al.* (1994) argue that in terms of survival it is sensible to be attracted to the familiar and to avoid the unfamiliar. Experience tells us that the familiar is safe whereas the unfamiliar could be very dangerous. Even very young babies prefer a familiar to an unfamiliar face, lending support to the evolutionary view that we may have a genetically based preference for people whom we know well.

Similarity

'Birds of a feather flock together' is a well-known saying that has a considerable ring of truth to it. Studies show that friends tend to be similar in many personal characteristics, including age, sex, marital status, ethnicity, personality traits, intelligence, attitudes and values. It will hardly surprise you that in same-sex friendships a similarity in preferred activities, pastimes and interests is especially important.

Byrne and his colleagues conducted many laboratory studies in which participants were requested to complete a questionnaire concerning their personal characteristics. They were then shown the questionnaire answers of another person and asked about their personal feelings towards this stranger. The questionnaires shown to the participants were, in fact, fabricated ones, manipulated to adjust the degree of similarity between that of the bogus (invented) person and the participant. From the results of these 'bogus stranger' studies, as they became known, Byrne (1971) formulated the **law of attraction**, which states that there is a direct linear relationship between the level of attraction and the proportion of similar attitudes.

Commentary

Byrne's studies have been criticised on the basis of their lack of ecological validity; that is, they do not reflect the way in which people in their everyday lives judge others and choose them as friends. As Duck (1995) points out, strangers don't make a habit of providing you with a written list of their attitudes. In real life we are cautious about how much we reveal and we are well aware that others are equally cautious. We therefore have to work out whether or not someone shares our attitudes. In the process we discover other characteristics about that person which may, in turn, influence our liking for them and theirs for us. Duck argues that the initial process of assessing our attraction to someone is not simply a case of matching their attitudes with ours. Rather, it is a process of each party communicating what they wish to reveal.

Another criticism is offered by Murstein (1976), who has pointed out that participants were given very limited information about the bogus stranger and had nothing except the questionnaire responses by which to judge them. This may have exaggerated the extent to which people use similarity to judge others.

Additional evidence

Nevertheless, **field studies** do tend to confirm the importance of similarity, especially similarity in attitudes. Byrne himself looked to everyday life situations to validate his findings. He found that bank managers were more generous in their allocation of loans to those people with similar attitudes, and that even white racists express liking for blacks who have similar attitudes. Kendel (1978) analysed the friendship patterns of more than 1,800 adolescents between the ages of 13 and 18 and found that 'best' friends were similar in terms of age, religion, ethnic group and family income and that they shared the same leisure interests.

The effects of similarity in different kinds of relationships

Similarity of attitudes and values is particularly important in the development of friendships and the more important the attitude is to the individual, the more it will influence the choice of friend. In the study by Kendel (1978) mentioned above, friends tended to have similar attitudes towards drug use but not necessarily towards parents and teachers.

When it comes to marriage, findings are not entirely consistent. Buss (1985) found that married and engaged couples tend to be matched in terms of intelligence, social class, attitudes and characteristics such as degree of smoking and alcohol consumption, and these findings have been confirmed by several similar studies. Nevertheless, there is evidence that romance can sometimes override attitude differences. Gold *et al.* (1984) demonstrated that, on occasions, 'love is blind'. They found that when men were given the impression that an attractive woman fancied them, they tended to misperceive her attitudes as being similar to their own, even though they were not. This study, set as it was in a laboratory using rather artificial conditions, again lacks ecological validity and tells us little about whether romantic relationships between very different people are likely to last. Nevertheless, it is possible that in increasingly mobile and multicultural societies, similarity is not as strong a factor as it used to be. In the Western world, there has been a steady increase in interethnic marriages. That said, the popular fictional notion that very dissimilar people can fall deeply in love and live happily ever after is not one that is reflected in real life. Evidence suggests that most stable marriages are those between couples who are similar (Cattell and Nesselrode, 1967).

Matching by relative attractiveness

In real life, it is a predicable finding that people tend to be matched in terms of physical attractiveness – the so-called **matching hypothesis**. Although artificially contrived studies do not always bear this out (for example, Walster *et al.*'s (1966) 'blind date' study discussed in the next section and in detail in Chapter 9), research outside the laboratory consistently shows this to be the case (e.g. Feingold, 1988). Several studies have looked at the physical attractiveness ratings of newly-weds or dating couples and found that each member of the pair tends to be similar in level of attractiveness. For example, Silverman (1971) conducted a field study in which researchers observed couples in bars and similar places and found, as expected, that they shared similar levels of attractiveness. Indeed, most of us quite automatically take account of this from our earliest romantic encounters. There may be a stunningly good-looking person at a party but if we consider ourselves to be 'average', the chances are we won't bother to chat them up because we know it would probably be time-wasting; and, worse still, we would risk rejection.

Perhaps more surprisingly, matching tends to apply to friendships as well as romantic relationships. In a field study, McKillip and Riedel (1983) observed pairs in real-life settings such as bars, assessed each on level of attraction and then asked them whether they were friends or lovers. If they were lovers they were then asked how strong and committed was their relationship. Both friends and lovers tended to be matched on physical attractiveness but the more casual lovers were less likely than the committed ones to be closely matched.

Exceptions to the similarity rule

The relationship between attraction and similarity is fairly robust, but there are exceptions.

• If individuals have very low self-esteem, so that they don't like themselves very much, then neither do they like those whom they perceive as being similar to them (Leonard, 1975).

- In situations where there is a great deal of uncertainty and confusion we may prefer to seek out people different from ourselves, perhaps in the hope that they can provide us with new information and offer a different perspective.
- Proximity is more important than similarity. Newcomb (1961), in a variation of his original study, deliberately pitted similarity against proximity. He offered students free accommodation if they were prepared to have shared rooms allocated to them. He then deliberately paired room-mates who were very different in terms of factors such as attitudes, interests, religion, background and area of study. Despite their differences, these couples generally formed firm friendships. While we are unlikely to seek out people who do not share our interests, it is not unusual to get on well with them once we do encounter them. For instance, if, through work, we meet people who are much older or younger, or who have very different attitudes and opinions from our own, we may enjoy experiencing a new outlook on life.

Is similarity or difference influential?

Notice that the studies we have examined show a *correlational relationship* between similarity and friendship. As discussed at the beginning of Chapter 1, this does not necessarily mean that we are attracted to another person because they are similar to us. Rosenbaum (1986) contends that social psychologists have overestimated the role of similarity of attitudes in interpersonal relations. In his **repulsion hypothesis**, he argues that we don't necessarily like people who share our attitudes but we do *dislike those whose attitudes differ greatly from ours*. He suggests that when we choose a long-term partner, we first eliminate all those whose attitudes contrast with our own and then select more or less randomly from the remainder.

In effect, studies do not support the idea that it is only dissimilarity that matters. Smeaton *et al.* (1989) kept the number of dissimilar attitudes of a bogus stranger the same but varied the number of similar attitudes. They found that, contrary to the repulsion hypothesis, the proportion of similar attitudes did have an effect. Nevertheless, Rosenbaum's contention has been of value in focusing attention on the influence of attitude dissimilarity. Evidence does indicate that disparate attitudes do have a slightly greater effect than do similar attitudes (Chapman, 1992).

Byrne *et al.* (1986) suggest, in their **proportional hypothesis**, a two-stage process in which the first stage is the same as that suggested by the repulsion hypothesis but the second stage differs. They propose that when we meet someone new we initially reject as potential friends all those who have very dissimilar attitudes to our own and from the remainder we select as friends those people with whom we share similar attitudes.

Why is similarity important?

- Byrne (1971) argues persuasively that people who agree with our attitudes bolster our self-esteem by making our own view of the world appear accurate, reasonable and worthy of respect. In this sense, similar people provide us with *direct reinforcement*. Byrne does allow for the fact that similar people are not always reinforcing – they may be boring – but in general, they are.
- There are few things quite as rewarding as being liked by others. Since we tend to assume that people who share our attitudes will like us, we like them.
- In a practical sense, we do tend to have considerable opportunities for meeting people who share our attitudes and interests. These encounters are liable to be positive, increasing the chances that a friendship will develop.
- It is easier to communicate with people who are similar to us. Being with them gives us a feeling of unity and a sense of belonging. We can relax and enjoy their company. We also anticipate that future meetings will be enjoyable and free from anxiety and conflict.

Physical attraction

To quote from a novel by David Lodge, 'Blessed are the good looking for they shall have fun'. There is little doubt that, no matter how unfair it is, being physically attractive makes people more popular, and that this applies not only in the obvious arena of sexual relationships but in friendships too.

In a now classic, though somewhat ethically dubious study, Walster *et al.* (1966) conducted a huge blind date experiment in which, for one evening, male and female students were paired randomly (with the exception that the man had to be taller than the woman). Before the date, students completed questionnaires concerning their interests, attitudes and personality. Unknown to them, they were rated by four independent judges in terms of their physical attraction. In an interval during the evening, males and females were temporarily separated and asked to give a written rating of their date. It was found that characteristics such as personality, intelligence, interests and self-esteem made little difference to the ratings. The only significant predictor of how highly people were rated was their physical attractiveness. (This study is one of the key research summaries in Chapter 9.)

The effect of physical attraction is extremely pervasive. Even young children prefer their physically attractive peers and consider that unattractive children are unfriendly and aggressive (Dion and Berscheid, 1974). Teachers rate attractive children as more intelligent than unattractive ones even when they have identical school records. Clearly it is not only in Hollywood that being attractive is a great advantage.

Nevertheless, although attractive people are generally more popular, extreme beauty can have its disadvantages. Exceptionally attractive people tend to have fewer than average same-sex friends and are liable to be judged vain, self-centred and unsympathetic (Dermer and Thiel, 1975). The ideal is to be very attractive but not exceptionally so.

Why is physical attraction important?

- The most obvious reason (but perhaps not the most important one) is the aesthetic pleasure derived from a drop-dead gorgeous face and body.
- Many studies indicate that we assume that good-looking people are more confident, happy, intelligent, warm and self-fulfilled than are their plainer counterparts. It is therefore assumed that their company is likely to be more stimulating.
- We gain considerable prestige from being associated with and 'chosen' by a glamorous companion, even when the relationship is not a romantic one. We may also assume that an attractive person is influential and this could, in turn, be advantageous to us.

1 Suggest three reasons why proximity may be important in the establishment of relationships.
2 Explain what is meant by the law of attraction.
3 Byrne conducted a series of studies based on a 'bogus stranger'. Explain why these studies may lack ecological validity.
4 Suggest two situations in which similarity may *not* lead to attraction.
5 Describe and evaluate one study that demonstrates the importance of physical attractiveness in the development of romantic relationships.
6 Describe some psychological evidence that disproves the saying 'Opposites attract'.

Reciprocal liking

Another factor that is an influence on our attraction to others is the extent to which they like us. In general, we like people who like us and dislike those who dislike us. In other words, we return or *reciprocate* people's feelings for us.

Backman and Secord (1959) found that if participants in a discussion group were led to believe that certain group members liked them, they were likely to choose these people to form a smaller group with them in a later session.

The belief that someone likes you can operate as a **self-fulfilling prophecy**, transforming the belief into actual reality. Curtis and Miller (1986) gave some participants the false impression that the people with whom they were having a discussion liked them very much. These participants more frequently expressed agreement, disclosed more personal information about themselves and had a generally more positive attitude than did participants who were not led to believe they were liked. This works as a self-fulfilling prophecy in the following manner. The belief that a person likes you makes you behave positively towards them. This makes them like you and respond by being positive towards you, which leads you to like them even more. So the belief that they like you has become a fact.

Interestingly, the people we most like are those who initially dislike us and then change their mind and come to like us (the so-called loss–gain situation). These people are actually preferred to people who have liked us all along (Aronson and Linder, 1965). The people we like least are those who like us initially but then begin to dislike us.

Qualifications and exceptions to principle of reciprocal liking

We are not completely indiscriminate when people express or indicate a liking for us.

- Sigall and Aronson (1969) found that male participants who were led to believe that a group of women liked them only reciprocated these feelings when the women were physically attractive, not when they were unattractive.
- Berscheid and Walster (1969) point out that if someone who likes us tells us things about ourselves which do not correspond to our self-concept, we will not return their liking. For example, if Chris says, 'you're great, so outgoing and fun loving' when you consider yourself to be introverted and shy, you will not value this opinion nor like Chris for expressing it.

Why is reciprocal liking important?

Basically, we like to be liked and would not find it rewarding to form a relationship with anyone who has a negative opinion of us. Being liked bolsters our self-esteem, makes us feel valued and therefore offers *positive reinforcement* (is rewarding).

Complementarity

Winch (1958) argued that some people are attracted to each other because each *complements* the needs of the other. For example, a dominant person may prefer a submissive partner and vice versa. Despite this popular notion that opposites attract, there is little evidence that it is actually true, despite its being investigated by many psychologists (e.g. O'Leary and Smith, 1991). The rule of similarity is far more likely to apply, especially in friendship.

Nevertheless, it is possible that complementarity of *resources* may have some role to play in the later stages of a relationship if not in its formation. If a couple has different skills, for example, Chris is good at decorating and ironing while Nicky is a proficient car mechanic and cook, then as a relationship develops, each individual may concentrate on their own areas and they will come to be mutually dependent. But whether or not this is so, it still lends no support to the idea that *personalities* of people in a relationship are opposite to one another, nor is it relevant to the *formation* of relationships.

Competence

On the whole, we prefer people who are socially skilled, intelligent and competent over those who are not. In fact, although good looks may be the magnet that attracts us in the first place, once a relationship is underway, intelligence may be more important. Indeed, if someone is intelligent they may be assessed as being physically attractive due to the *halo effect*, i.e. that people who are judged positively on one characteristic are also judged positively on others. There is a stereotype that 'what is beautiful is good'; this constitutes the reverse of this, that what is good is beautiful.

One particular area of incompetence we have little time for is people who are boring. Leary *et al.* (1986) found that interesting participants were rated as more popular, friendly, enthusiastic and less impersonal than boring speakers.

Exceptions to a liking for competence

- Hagen and Kahn (1975) discovered that although men expressed a preference for a competent woman over an incompetent one when shown a hypothetical profile of her, in reality it was quite another story. Presented with actual women, men no longer preferred the competent one. This study highlights the constant problem of the ecological validity of studies. What is found from materials such as questionnaires does not always reflect real-life attitudes and opinions.
- There is such a thing as being 'too perfect'. Most of us can appreciate that, much as we may like accomplished individuals, if they have no weak spots or flaws at all we become exasperated and irritated by them. Aronson and Worchel (1966) arranged a scenario in which an exceptionally talented individual made a minor blunder by spilling coffee. This greatly improved his popularity, probably because he suddenly became 'human' – the so-called 'pratfall effect'. However when a fairly incompetent individual did the same, he became even less popular.

Why is competence important?

In general, socially skilled, competent, intelligent people are rewarding to be with whatever their particular area of competence.

1 Imagine you are designing a building which will house forty students. What factors should be taken into account so that both privacy and the opportunity for meeting people can be afforded to all the residents?

2 Mnemonics are devices that help us to remember things, and are particularly useful when trying to remember a list. For example, the well-known mnemonic Richard Of York Gave Battle In Vain helps us remember the colours of the rainbow. The important factors determining relationship formation are proximity, similarity, physical attraction, reciprocal liking, complementarity, competence. Take the initial letters and invent an appropriate mnemonic which will be helpful in exams.

3 What is the 'matching hypothesis'? With the help of the *Psychology Review* article mentioned in the section on further reading below, think of a way in which you could use a correlational design to test the hypothesis. (Correlational designs are discussed at the beginning of Chapter 1.) Make sure that your study is ethical.

Summary

The major factors that determine the onset of a relationship are:

- *Proximity*. The closer two people live or work and the more they interact with each other and become *familiar*, the more likely they are to become friends or lovers.
- *Similarity*. The more similar two people are, especially in terms of attitudes and interests, the more likely they are to form a relationship.
- *Physical attractiveness*. People of similar attractiveness tend to pair off. This applies to friendships and particularly to sexual relationships.
- *Reciprocal liking*. We like those people who like us and dislike those people who dislike us.

- *Competence*. We like people who are reasonably competent and socially skilled but who are not 'too perfect'.

It has been suggested that people who are very different may be attracted because they complement each other, each satisfying the other's needs, but the evidence for this is weak.

Further reading

Brigham, J.C. (1991) *Social Psychology* (2nd edn), New York: HarperCollins. Chapter 8 covers the basic ideas discussed in this chapter, with some aspects (such as attractiveness) covered in a little more detail and applied to everyday circumstances.

Wadeley, A. (1996) Blind date research revisited, *Psychology Review* 3 (1), 6–7. This is an article based on Walster *et al.* (1966), given more recent research, and commenting on ways in which you can carry out a workable practical for your coursework.

4

Theories of interpersonal attraction

◼ Learning theory
◆ Social exchange theory
◼ Equity theory
◢ Sociobiology

In Chapter 3 we saw that certain factors, in particular proximity, similarity and physical attractiveness, are important in the formation of friendship and romantic relationships. In this chapter we will explore some of the theories that seek to explain *why* these and other factors may be of importance in the formation, maintenance and perhaps dissolution of such relationships.

Learning theory

Byrne and Clore (1970), in their **reinforcement–affect theory**, argue that both **classical conditioning** and **operant conditioning** help to forge friendships and romantic liaisons. Classical conditioning involves learning by association, so that a neutral stimulus produces an emotional response. We may learn to associate the sound of a dentist's drill with fear, even though the sound has never hurt us. Operant conditioning involves learning by consequences, so that we are more likely to do things that are reinforced and less likely to do things that that are punished.

The effect of classical conditioning on liking

In terms of classical conditioning, we like people with whom we associate enjoyment and satisfaction, even if they are not directly responsible for these positive experiences. If we meet people under pleasant circumstances, such as seeing them regularly at our local pub, we are more likely to be attracted to them than to those whom we meet under disagreeable situations such as at a tedious series of committee meetings. Evidence to support this is offered by a study by Veitch and Griffith (1976), who demonstrated that people who interacted with a stranger against a background news programme of all good news rated the stranger more positively than those interacting with a stranger while listening to a news broadcast full of depressing news items.

Many similar studies have demonstrated that a variety of negative and positive circumstances, such as the mood of a film or even pleasing or disagreeable lighting, influence the degree to which we are attracted to someone (Gouaux, 1971; Baron and Thomley, 1992). So it is perhaps worth bearing this in mind next time you're planning a romantic meal.

Clore and Byrne (1974) argue that when we experience enjoyable shared activities with other people this creates in us a positive emotional response; in other words, positive *affect* which strengthens our desire to be with those individuals. If they have also enjoyed the experience, the positive emotional response and desire for continued interaction will be mutual.

The effect of operant conditioning on liking

Operant conditioning explains the fact that we like people who reward us and dislike those who punish us. Rewards may include scintillating company and a friendly, helpful and cheerful disposition. Punishment may be in the form of disapproval of our values or simply being a rather tedious and boring companion.

Applying reinforcement–affect theory

We can interpret the effects of proximity, similarity and physical attractiveness partly in terms of classical and partly in terms of operant conditioning.

Proximity: when we interact with people on a regular basis because we live or work near them, the opportunities for positive easy-going interactions and social exchanges are plentiful. On the other hand, if the interactions are negative, it also accounts for the intense dislike that sometimes occurs between neighbours.

Similarity: when people are similar to us, they offer powerful rewards in terms of boosting our self-esteem by approval of our opinions and values. In addition, it is highly probable that we can enjoy joint activities with those who share our interests. In contrast, we find it very unpleasant to be with people who disagree with us, who criticise our beliefs and challenge our judgements, thereby threatening our self-esteem.

Physical attraction: physically attractive people offer us the direct reward of aesthetic pleasure, and the indirect one of being admired for our association with a good-looking individual.

Theorists also use learning theory to account for the changing nature of relationships. In the early stages, rewards are likely to include the novelty and interest associated with the excitement of a new friendship. As things 'settle down', then familiarity and the freedom to relax in the company of someone you know well becomes rewarding. The actual rewards involved in friendship as opposed to a romantic relationship may be different but as long they are reinforcing, the relationship will continue. Relationships begin to fail when these rewards diminish and possibly cease, perhaps because people no longer have rewarding experiences such as interesting conversations, affectionate hugs and enjoyable evenings out, and instead begin to take each other for granted.

Evaluation

Critics point to several limitations of learning theory as a *sole* explanation for the relationship formation, maintenance and break-down.

Firstly, there are occasions in which shared misery creates a sense of solidarity that forms the basis for friendship (Kenrick and Johnson, 1979). This would appear to contradict the principle that by classical conditioning we dislike those people whom we have encountered in unpleasant or boring situations. It is possible that under these circumstances, friendships are formed because of the rewards gained by working together under adverse circumstances, but this underscores the problems of using this theory to *predict* whether or not a positive relationship will form. Real-life relationships are complex and it is not always easy to determine exactly what is reinforcing for different individuals. It is also difficult to decipher the relative importance of operant and classical conditioning when they would not lead to the same outcome.

Secondly, this theory tends to view people as essentially selfish, engaging in relationships which are rewarding to them, either directly or through social rewards. However, as Argyle (1988) points out, in close relationships in which people have genuine concern for each other, it may be rewarding simply to see the other person rewarded.

Thirdly, learning theory may not be able to account for all forms of bonding. For example, Hill (1970), who studied family relationships over several generations, believes that blood ties are not based on reinforcement. For example, sociobiologists (described later in this chapter), who are concerned with the evolutionary basis for social behaviour, argue that blood ties are based on an innate, in-built propensity to support and cherish those to whom we are related, regardless of how directly rewarding those relationships are.

Fourthly, the evidence in support of the theory is based largely on laboratory studies, such as the study by Veitch and Griffith (1976) cited above. These types of study are unlikely to reflect the complexity of the circumstances in which we meet people in everyday life.

Despite these limitations and criticisms, the learning theory approach to relationships does account for some important research findings. As we have already seen, it accounts for the findings on the importance of proximity, similarity and physical attractiveness in influencing the formation of relationships. There can also be little doubt that rewarding experiences help to cement a relationship, and when these rewards diminish or cease altogether, the relationship is liable to run into trouble. Because this theory is limited rather than incorrect, it has formed the basis for the next two theories that we shall consider below: social exchange theory and equity theory.

Social exchange theory

Social exchange theory (SET) is an economic model of human behaviour with a very simple fundamental premise. It is economic insofar as it proposes that relationships are based on the exchange of rewards and costs between the people concerned and that the most satisfying and long-lasting relationships are those that involve the greatest rewards at the lowest cost. It applies to all kinds of relationships: those with your boss, teacher, friend or lover.

Over the years, the basic ideas of social exchange theory have been modified and extended. The simplest way to view it is to look at three major factors that influence the satisfaction of a relationship: *profits*, *alternatives* and *investments*.

Profits

Homans (1961) proposed that before embarking on a relationship, we weigh up the past, present and possible future rewards and costs, and if we judge it to be profitable, the relationship will go ahead. If, on the other hand, we assess that a loss may be incurred, the relationship is likely to be a non-starter. This principle applies to both parties, so the relationship has to be *mutually beneficial* in order to form and survive. As in economics, a profit or loss is calculated by rewards minus costs. Homans (1961) defined rewards very generally, as anything a person feels is valuable, so rewards may include compliments, entertaining company and material gifts. Costs can also take almost any form, since they are anything which someone considers to be unpleasant, such as arguments, irritating habits or feeling obliged to cook a meal every night.

To sum up, according to Homans, we calculate profit or loss by analysing the benefits and costs and seek to gain the best outcome for ourselves – that is, maximum benefits with minimum costs.

Research evidence supports the idea that in intimate relationships, greater rewards are associated with longer endurance. Dating couples who start out having many rewarding interactions are less likely to break up than those who start with fewer rewards (Lloyd *et al.*, 1984).

The picture for costs is not quite so straightforward. According to Rusbult (1983), who has analysed costs and rewards in intimate relationships, during the 'honeymoon' period of such a relationship, costs don't really come into play. For about the first three months, costs tended to be ignored and therefore did not affect the degree of satisfaction with the relationship. Only later were increasing costs related to decreased satisfaction. As the theory would predict, in long-standing, cohabiting relationships, whether gay, lesbian or hetero-sexual, high rewards and low costs are associated with the greatest fulfilment.

Alternatives

Thibaut and Kelley (1959) suggested that when we calculate whether or not a relationship is profitable and therefore satisfactory, we base it not only on the *actual* rewards and costs but on *comparisons* with other rewards and costs. We use two dimensions by which we make these assessments: *comparison level* and *comparison level for alternatives*.

The **comparison level** is the amount of rewards we think we deserve from the relationship. This is based on standards derived from social norms and personal expectations. Our comparison level, therefore, depends on our past experiences in relationships and what we've come to expect based on what we see in other relationships, including those in books and films. Because we are constantly experiencing new relationships, our comparison level is liable to change over time. We may not understand why Sue seems content with her husband who does not get home until ten every night, having gone to the pub after work. But this becomes more understandable when we know that Sue was previously married to a man who was violent and did not want children, whereas in her present marriage her husband has been enthusiastic about being a father and is a good material provider. Similarly with other relationships, we are more likely to be content with a strict but fair boss if we have previously had to tolerate a bad-tempered, unfair superior rather than an easy-going, tolerant one.

The comparison level of any one person is closely related to their self-esteem. People with high self-esteem have a relatively high comparison level for interpersonal relationships – they expect to have relationships that provide a high profit level. In contrast, people with low self-esteem and therefore a low comparison level settle for relationships that show little profit or even a loss, because this is all they expect and/or believe they deserve.

The **comparison level for alternatives** is the amount of costs and rewards we believe are available from alternative relationships. Thibaut and Kelley recognised that we cannot consider rewards and costs in isolation but must take account of the context of what else is available. All relationships, but especially sexual ones, entail limitations being put on other relationships. If we spend lots of time with one group of friends, it inevitably limits the time available for others, and if we are in an intimate relationship, the usual (but not invariable) expectation is that we no longer have sexual relationships with other people. Chris might be quite content in a relationship that is comfortable but has never been desperately romantic until he is 'swept off his feet' by a new work colleague. It has been suggested that some people remain in very unsatisfactory relationships because they believe that the alternative of being alone is worse.

Just as the amount of commitment we make to a relationship depends to some extent on the alternatives, so the commitment influences the way we perceive the alternatives. When developing a relationship, individuals gradually close themselves off from attractive alternatives. Simpson *et al.* (1990) found that people who were dating someone viewed members of the opposite sex as less attractive than did those who were not courting. Johnson and Rusbult (1989) arranged for highly committed individuals to interact with an attractive member of the opposite sex on a computer dating exercise. They found that these individuals were particularly derogatory about these potential threats to their relationship. Duck (1994) argued that the state of a current relationship helps determine how attractive the alternatives appear. He points out that there are always alternative partners in an objective sense but we only notice them when we are fed up with what we have. Those who are committed are less interested in alternatives and see them as relatively unattractive.

Despite this, it should be noted that an attractive person is still one of the major contributors to the breakup of a relationship (Buunk, 1987).

Rusbult (1983) adds a further element to SET by suggesting that commitment to a relationship does not only depend on outcomes and available alternatives but on the *amount of investment* that has been made. Once a well-established relationship begins to pall we can pack our things, collect the cat and go – but it's not that easy. We have put time, effort and money into the relationship. We share possessions and mutual friends. We may have given up career opportunities and other romantic alternatives. We may also feel that we have given our partner the 'best years of our life' and now have less to offer someone else. According to Rusbult, the greater the investment, the greater the commitment, and the more likely we are to stay. Investments, then not only increase commitment but serve *to stabilise* a relationship.

Evaluation

We have already noted several research studies that lend support to this model. In addition, other studies have shown that it does effectively predict how long a premarital relationship will last (Cate and Lloyd, 1992) and helps to account for why people return to an abusive relationship (Rusbult and Martz, 1995). Nevertheless, despite this support, there are some limitations and criticisms of this approach.

Firstly, most of the research has been conducted on short-term relationships with student samples and little on married relationships over a wider population. Secondly, this model says very little about individual differences in people's willingness to commit to a relationship. Commitment may be more dependent on a person's willingness to trust another based on earlier experiences than on the rewards and investments.

Thirdly, when considering the comparison level for alternatives, Pennington (1986) pointed out that SET does not predict the level at which a relationship has become so unsatisfactory that a person will leave, despite having no other relationship to which to turn. Pennington suggests that SET needs to include a notion of *general expectation* that specifies the minimum which people expect from a relationship. In other words, it ought to specify the level of satisfaction below which a person would leave even if there was no new relationship.

Fourthly, and probably the most fundamental criticism of SET, is the idea that in many relationships, but especially in long-term sexual ones, people do not behave like level-headed accountants motivated only by maximising their profits. Where in this approach are the ecstasies and agonies of falling in and out of love? Intimate relationships, especially at the beginning and end, are characterised by intense emotions and extravagant and impulsive actions which have no mention here. As Berscheid (1983) pointed out, attraction as a mental calculation has received considerable attention; attraction as raw emotion has received considerably less.

Nevertheless, this approach does offer a plausible account for much of the time spent in a romantic relationship as well as for the course of other relationships, such as those with friends, work colleagues and neighbours. Ultimately, though, some psychologists reject outright the notion implicit in this approach that true altruism plays no part in human relationships. They do not believe that relationships never involve freely and lovingly giving yourself to someone else in the absence of reward (e.g. Rubin, 1973).

Imagine you are a student in the sixth form at school with four very close friends. At the end of your school career, you and three of your friends leave to go to university in towns quite far apart and the fourth friend gets a job locally. After one term away, you all meet up for a longed-for reunion in a local pub. In terms of social exchange theory, how have the rewards and costs in your relationships now changed since you were all at school together? Think about the arrangements you now need to make in order to see each other, the things you have to talk about, your shared experiences. Which costs have increased and decreased; which rewards have increased or decreased? How do these 'old' relationships compare with alternative relationships you have now made? What aspects are better and what are worse? (Consider the value of reminiscence, of novelty and of familiarity.)

Go a bit further through your lives. You all form new friendships, you all have romances, some of you get married, some have children. Again, in terms of rewards and costs, what is likely to change? Is it possible to make suggestions, albeit very tentative ones, about the circumstances under which people stay in touch or drift apart?

Progress exercise

Equity theory

Equity theory, formulated by Walster *et al.* (1978), is a specific version of how social exchange operates in interpersonal relationships and is derived from Homans' (1961) original social exchange theory. The equity principle states that people will only consider a relationship to be 'fair' and satisfactory if what they gain from a relationship reflects what they put in. Equity is not the same as equality. If one partner puts more into the relationship, they should get more out of it. If this is not the case, they feel exploited or that they are taking unfair advantage of their partner.

Equity theory, therefore, predicts that a relationship in which a partner is overbenefited or underbenefited will not be a happy one. Underbenefited individuals tend to feel angry, resentful and deprived. Those who are overbenefited may feel guilty and uncomfortable. Although both imbalances are unhappy states, it is not surprising that being underbenefited leads to greater dissatisfaction than being over-benefited (Hatfield *et al.*, 1982). People prefer to receive too much rather than too little, even if it makes them feel uneasy.

Hatfield *et al.* (1985) have devised the Hatfield Global Measure in order to assess levels of equity. People are asked to assess what they contribute to and what they derive from their relationship compared to the input and output of their partner and whether, as a consequence, they deem their relationship to be a fair one. Research evidence supports equity theory. Hatfield *et al.* (1972) asked over five hundred college men and women involved in romantic relationships to judge how equitable this relationship was. As predicted by the theory, after three months, students in inequitable relationships were more likely to have ended them.

Equity theory helps explain the matching hypothesis (mentioned in Chapter 3) – the finding that, on the whole, people form sexual relationships with someone of equivalent attractiveness (not just physical attractiveness). Physical attractiveness is one important factor used to decide whether a relationship is equitable. Couples who match each other in physical attractiveness have equity in one of the important characteristics of a sexual relationship. If a physically unattractive older woman is partnered with a very attractive younger man, we assume that the older woman must be contributing some-thing extra to the relationship, since on the surface it is inequitable. We may make the not unreasonable guess that she is very rich.

Equity seems to be especially important in the early stages of a relationship. Once the relationship is well established, partners tend to trust the other's good intentions and do not monitor the relative contributions too closely (Cate *et al.*, 1988).

Men and women appear to have different attitudes and responses to inequity. Hatfield *et al.* (1985) found that women are more distressed about being overbenefited whereas men are more uncomfortable about being underbenefited. This may reflect other research evidence indicating that in general men care more about rewards, whereas women are more concerned for the welfare of others, especially those in their care. Prins *et al.* (1992) found that women but not men in inequitable relationships are likely to engage in extra-marital affairs, presumably in order to give what they perceive to be a more equitable balance to the relationship.

Evaluation

As with social exchange theory, there is a considerable body of evidence, some of it already mentioned, that supports equity theory. Nevertheless, there are several circumstances in which equity is not the only, or even arguably the main, factor that needs to be considered.

Firstly, Cate *et al.* (1988) believe that it is the absolute level of rewards rather than fairness that predicts the satisfaction in love relationships. In general, the more good things are being received from a relationship, the better we feel about it. Rewards such as love, status and sexual satisfaction are more important to us than perfect equity in the exchange of rewards.

Secondly, there is evidence to suggest that not all individuals put an equal value on equity. Equity is certainly important to some individuals – those said to be high in **exchange orientation** – but this does not apply to everyone. Buunk and VanYperen (1991) believe that some people, said to be low in exchange orientation, really don't mind about equity.

Thirdly, Clark and Mills (1979) argue that romantic relationships do not work on exchange principles at all, since they are *communal* relationships – relationships in which people gain satisfaction by responding to each other's needs. According to these theorists, very close relationships involve a commitment that is selfless and transcends economic considerations. Indeed, research conducted by Clark and Mills (1979) indicates that people in the early stages of a relationship interpret the need to reciprocate as a sign that the other person is not interested in a romantic liaison.

Fourthly, cross-cultural studies indicate that even if the equity principle is the norm for relationships in some societies, it is not universal but a characteristic of individualistic societies. Berman *et al.* (1985) asked Indian and American students to decide which of two workers, a needy one and an excellent one, should receive a bonus payment. The American students tended to choose the excellent worker, as predicted by equity theory. The Indian students, however, were more inclined to allocate the extra resources on the basis of need. Moghaddam *et al.* (1993) suggest two possibilities to account for these findings. It is possible that in societies in which abject poverty exists and need is therefore very visible, the norm of justice is based on meeting these needs rather than on equity. Alternatively, it may be rooted in the fact that Indian society is very interdependent, whereas American culture stresses the importance of individual achievement and personal independence (individualistic relationships). In the group-orientated Indian society, the norm may be that resources should be allocated on the basis of group need rather than on the basis of individual equity as in competitive American society. The basic problem with the theory of equity is that, like much other work in this area, it is based mainly on studies of people raised in Western cultures. It may not therefore be applicable to other societies.

Sociobiology

We now turn from economics to evolution for an explanation of who chooses whom in relationships. Unlike the previous theories, this one does not seek to explain the choices we make in all relationships, but what people seek in heterosexual attachments.

Sociobiology applies the principles of evolution to the understanding of social behaviour. The theory argues that the behaviour of all animals has evolved so that it maximises the likelihood that individuals will pass on their genes to future generations. In human terms, this means that both women and men unconsciously behave in ways that promote conception, birth and survival of their offspring. In pursuit of this end, the optimal mating behaviour differs dramatically between men and women (Trivers, 1972). Since a man can, in theory, impregnate many women within a short time and will only waste some easily replaceable sperm if sexual intercourse does not result in pregnancy, it is in his interest to be promiscuous and seek out good child-bearers. A woman, who has to invest a great deal more in bearing each child than does a man, is likely to be far more choosy when selecting a mate. She will be coy, take her time and choose a man who can provide for her and her infant, perhaps an older man who is established in his career.

Research does support the fact that men tend to give a high priority to youth and beauty (which are taken as indicators of child-bearing potential) while women prefer older men of higher educational and occupational status (indicative of good earning potential). For example, men are attracted to women with a low waist-to-hip ratio (with the waist smaller than the hip!) and this is related to child-bearing potential (Singh, 1993). Buss (1989), in an extensive study of thirty-seven cultures (in thirty-three countries), analysed the results of more than 10,000 questionnaires asking respondents to rate a number of factors such as age, intelligence and sociability, for their importance in a sexual partner. Consistent with sociobiological theory, findings were that men valued physical attractiveness more than did women, while women were more likely than men to value good earning potential and high occupational status. In all the cultures both women and men preferred the man to be the older of the pair. It is worth noting however that gender differences in the importance of physical attraction are stronger when people estimate its importance (as in questionnaires) than when they actually interact with someone.

What about the intense emotions involved in falling in love? Kenrick and Trost (1989) believe that passionate love has evolved as an innate behaviour to ensure strong pair bonding and thereby a secure family unit in which to nurture the young. This may offer a more plausible account of romantic love than does the exchange model of level-headed calculation of assets.

Evaluation

We have looked at some evidence in favour of sociobiology; we will now consider the problems. The major limitation of sociobiological explanations in general is that they use hindsight to explain almost any behaviour in terms of why it has evolved. One important characteristic of a good theory is that it can be used to make predictions about the future, yet sociobiology has little predictive value. There are so many possibilities with regard to how behaviour may evolve that prediction becomes impossible.

Another significant problem is that it is extremely difficult to untangle the effects of culture from those of evolution. Despite Buss' work, there are significant historical and cultural differences in heterosexual mate selection. For example, men's preference for younger women was considerably greater in the past than it is now and is greater in traditional than in modern societies (Glenn, 1989). The difficulty of separating culture from evolution will always mean that sociobiology is likely to remain controversial.

More specifically, there is little evidence of a direct link between physical attractiveness and child-bearing potential. Attractiveness may be considered an indicator of youth and health but it is not a major indicator of child-bearing capacity. A plain woman can breed quite as well as a pretty one. It is also difficult to see how some specific hypotheses, for example, that of Cunningham (1986) that men prefer women with 'cute' features associated with babies (such as large, widely spaced eyes, small noses and small chins), tie in with men being attracted to women who are good child-bearers.

Although sociobiological theory remains speculative and controversial, it does serve to remind us that relationships fulfil an important biological function and satisfy such a basic need that it would be imprudent to dismiss entirely the role of biology.

Review exercise

1 In terms of learning theory, think of two factors that, in the course of everyday life, may lead to *positive* associations with another person and two factors that may give *negative* associations with someone whom you have just met. How do positive and negative associations affect the possibility of the formation of friendships?

2 How does learning theory account for the effect of proximity, similarity and physical attraction on the probability of friendship formation?

3 In terms of equity theory, what does it mean to be 'underbenefited' and 'overbenefited' in a relationship? What are the effects on the relationship of each of these conditions?

4 According to sociobiology, what basic factor controls the evolution of body and behaviour? How would a sociobiologist account for the different characteristics men and women look for in members of the opposite sex when seeking a sexual relationship?

Summary

- *Learning theory* applied to interpersonal relationships is known as the *reinforcement-affect theory*. Through classical conditioning, we like people with whom we associate pleasant occasions and are less likely to be attracted to those whom we associate with unpleasant circumstances. Although the theory undoubtedly has some basis in truth it is probably rather simplistic, not taking sufficient account of the two-way process of relationship formation.

- *Social exchange theory* is essentially an economic theory which proposes that we weigh up the benefits and costs of a relationship and if the benefits outweigh the costs the relationship will form and continue, but if it sustains a loss the relationship may be dissolved. Although there is research evidence to support this model, the most fundamental criticism is that people do not always level-headedly calculate costs and rewards: people are quite capable of loving and giving in the absence of reward.

- *Equity theory* is a form of exchange theory that includes a consideration of investment. It states that people expect to receive rewards commensurate with their investment; thus the more you put in, the more you expect to gain. If people get too much or too little (particularly the latter), they will be discontent. Critics point out that there are several circumstances in which equity is not the only, or even the main determinant of satisfaction.

- *Sociobiology* argues that behaviour has evolved so that it maximises our chances of propagating our genes. In heterosexual relationships men maximise these chances by mating with as many healthy child-bearing women as possible. Consequently, they are inclined towards promiscuity. Women have little to gain from indiscriminate matings and are very selective in their choice of mate, seeking out men who are likely to support them. Sociobiology has been criticised for emphasising the influence of evolution over that of learned, cultural preferences. The theory is speculative but does serve to remind us of the influence of biology in the basic process of reproduction.

Further reading

Cartwright, J. (1996) Choosing a mate, *Psychology Review* 3 (1). This article discusses the sociobiological approach to choosing a mate and considers the extent to which good looks do equal good genes. It covers some interesting research (which you may wish to replicate!) on the vital statistics of *Playboy* centrefolds.

Davis, S. (1990) Men as success objects and women as sex objects: a study of personal advertisements, *Sex Roles* 23 (1/2), 43–50. This article, which also takes a sociobiological approach and lends itself to replication for coursework, is covered in detail in Chapter 9.

Lippa, R.A. (1990) *Introduction to Social Psychology*, CA: Wadsworth. Chapter 11 covers all the theories discussed in this chapter in a very accessible way.

5

The maintenance and course of relationships

◼ Stage and filter models
◆ Evaluation of filter and stage theories

Stage and filter models

Relationships have beginnings, middles and sometimes endings. When considering the course taken by relationships, a number of social scientists have suggested that close relationships pass through a fixed series of stages. **Filter theories** attempt to explain the selection of partners in terms of a series of stages during which choices are successively narrowed down. Although these theories have been applied to friendships, the two filter theories discussed below (those of Kerckhoff and Davis and of Murstein) were based on research with dating couples and originally focused on the selection of a long-term partner, usually a spouse. Not all stage theories involve filtering. The third theory considered in this chapter is one such example: Levinger's theory looks at the stages involved in the life cycle of intimate relationships.

Kerckhoff and Davis: filter theory

Kerckhoff and Davis (1962) propose that during courtship people successively narrow down or 'filter out' those with whom they feel they would like to become more intimately involved. At the beginning and end of a seven-month longitudinal study, Kerckhoff and Davis asked student participants in dating relationships to complete questionnaires concerned with family values and the degree to which their own and their partner's needs were complementary. Complementary needs are those that fit together in a mutually satisfying way, as in the case of a partnership consisting of a dominant and a submissive individual.

In the second part of the study, the courting couples were also asked to estimate the progress of their relationship by saying whether, compared to seven months before, they thought the likelihood of their forming a permanent relationship was stronger, weaker or unchanged.

Based on the results of this study, Kerckhoff and Davis concluded that in the early stages of a relationship *social variables* such as class, religion and education are used as a filter, with people preferring others who are similar to themselves in these attributes. As the relationship moves on, agreement on *values* becomes important; and finally, complementary *personal traits* become a decisive factor. Notice that in order for a couple to be compatible, social attributes and values need to be *similar*, whereas personality traits need to be *complementary*.

Many of you may be surprised that personality traits were not taken into consideration right at the beginning of a relationship. Kerckhoff and Davis argued that in the early stages of a romantic relationship each partner is likely to have an idealised romantic picture of the other. The fact that they are wearing rose-coloured spectacles means that incompatibility is not acknowledged or even recognised. As the courtship progresses, more realism creeps in and compatibility in personality becomes a decisive factor.

To summarise, this filter model states that, in the first stage of courtship, similarity of opinions and attitudes is the operative filter and, in the later stages (after about eighteen months), psychological compatibility becomes the decisive factor. In these later stages, social factors have no influence, presumably because most of the partnerships in which values were incompatible have already been filtered out.

Evaluation of Kerckhoff and Davis' model

We will evaluate stage models in general at the end of this section, but with respect to this model, two specific problems are worth noting.

Firstly, attempts to replicate the findings of the original research have not been successful (Levinger *et al.*, 1970). Secondly, it is doubtful whether we choose partners on the basis of complementary needs. As noted in Chapter 4, although the notion that opposites attract seems plausible, it has not been generally supported by research evidence (e.g. O'Leary and Smith, 1991).

Murstein: stimulus-value-role (SVR) model

Murstein (1970) offered an alternative filter theory known as the **stimulus-value-role model**. This model suggests that the selection of an intimate partner occurs in three stages, at each of which certain options are filtered out and decisions made to maintain, deepen or end the relationship.

1 In the *stimulus stage* we assess the other person in terms of *physical attributes*. If either person fails to provide sufficient reinforcement, no more contact is sought. In everyday language, we decide whether or not we think someone is attractive, and if we do not 'fancy' them we make no overtures that could lead to romantic entanglements. People are generally attracted to those who are similar in age, appearance and ethnicity. At the stimulus stage, no interaction between the couple is required in order for the filtering to take place.

2 In the *value stage* we assess whether or not we have compatible values and attitudes. Particularly important are similarity in attitudes towards family life, religion, career, sex and the role of men and women in society. This stage requires at least verbal interaction and this, in turn, allows each party to examine more closely some of the stimulus variables, such as physical attractiveness and the ability to relate to others.

   Some couples will marry on the basis of stimulus and value similarity, but for most people this is not enough: if they are compatible so far, they move to the third stage.

3 During the *role stage* partners increasingly confide in each other and become aware of what they desire in a spouse and whether or not there is a role 'fit'. Roles themselves may be complementary (you sweep the chimney, I'll feed the rabbit) but *attitudes* towards roles need to be similar in order for the relationship to be harmonious.

Note that each of these sets of factors – physical stimuli, values, roles – has *some* influence throughout the courtship, but each one is said to be of paramount importance during only one stage.

Evaluation of Murstein's model

Stephen (1985) has criticised Murstein's model on the basis that, like similar models, it portrays matching as a process which occurs via mutual selection rather than something that is achieved through communication. Where opinions differ, rather than end the relationship, a couple may discuss, argue and influence each other until they become compatible. Simply establishing that similarity of attitudes exists now between a dating couple does not tell us whether or not they have *always* been similar in that respect.

Although Murstein disputes this, Stephen convincingly argues that SVR theory sees values, attitudes and beliefs as static (unchanging) characteristics rather than entities that are created or altered by interpersonal communication.

Levinger: stage theory model

Unlike the previous two models, Levinger's model does not discuss the processes by which we choose a partner but looks at the alterations that take place as a relationship changes in levels of intimacy. It embraces many types of relationship, such as friendship, which may be intimate but not necessarily romantic.

Levinger proposes five possible stages in the development of a close relationship:

A – acquaintance (attraction)
B – buildup
C – continuation (consolidation)
D – deterioration (decline)
E – ending

A – acquaintance. A relationship begins when people are mutually attracted and, as we have already seen, attraction depends largely on similarity in terms of age, social class and so on. A strong source of attraction at the beginning of a romantic relationship is erotic, passionate love. In certain relationships (for example, one between people who work together) the acquaintance stage may last indefinitely.

B – buildup. Buildup involves increasing interdependence. During this stage, the couple engage in increasing amounts of self-disclosure and there is a considerable amount of social exchange, both of pleasure and unpleasantness. Close relationships involve negative aspects, such as disputes and irritating habits, and rewarding ones such as affection and exchange of gifts.

C – continuation. The social norms having been established, the relationship may enter the continuation stage during which it becomes consolidated, and a commitment, such as marriage, may be made. In very long-term relationships the partners enmesh their lives and have many close ties. This stage differs from all the others in that it does not usually involve great intensity of emotion such as elation or rage. It is possible that once a relationship enters into a stable state the partners begin to take each other for granted. The underlying emotional depth of the relationship may not become apparent unless it is threatened. The continuation stage may last indefinitely or the relationship may go downhill.

D – deterioration. Relationships do not necessarily reach the deterioration stage but a large number do. Levinger (1976) used social exchange theory (discussed in Chapter 4) to predict whether a relationship will deteriorate. There are several factors that influence whether or not the relationship deteriorates: costs, rewards, alternatives and barriers to breakdown. Sometimes, however, breakdown is related to external events or factors.

E – ending. If costs increase, rewards decrease, if attractive alternatives are available and if the barriers to break up are not too high, deterioration is liable to lead to the last stage: the end.

Levinger noted that few relationships actually pass through all five stages. Many never get beyond acquaintance and most terminate at buildup, as one would expect in the majority of friendships.

Evaluation of filter and stage theories

One major problem with stage theories is that they portray a situation in which all relationships follow the same linear course in the same direction. However, both the stages themselves and their sequence may not be universal; each relationship is, to some extent, unique. A number of investigators suggest that the evidence for a fixed sequence of stages is not very convincing. (e.g. Leigh *et al.*, 1987). Surra and Huston (1987) asked newly-wed couples how their relationship had developed and discovered a wide varity of sequences. Brehm (1992) comments that, in light of this, rather than use the term 'stages', it is better to view the course of relationships as 'phases' that take place at different times for different couples.

Miell and Crogham (1996) have pointed out several other short-comings with stage theories. Firstly, they tend to portray a relationship where one active person makes selection decisions involving a passive partner. In reality, a relationship consists of two active people having discussions, making decisions and influencing each other. One example of such mutual influence is that we tend to form friendships only with people who like us and not with those who dislike us. Far from being passive, the actions of the other party have an impact on our reaction and on whether or not we wish to take the relationship any further. And of course this is reciprocal.

Secondly, there is such a huge diversity in types of relationships (especially friendships) that the generalisations made in these models may not accurately reflect the wide diversity in relationship development.

Thirdly, the experimental procedures involved in research on which these theories are based involve people being presented with artificial tasks, usually the completion of long questionnaires, that reveal very little about the complexity of real-life relationships.

With regard to filter theories in particular, Duck (1992) argues that they over-emphasise the role of thought in the selection process while ignoring the extent to which other processes, such as daily interactions, influence our feelings for other people. Whereas we may admire someone for their physical attractiveness and agree with their attitudes and values, they may irritate us intensely when they chatter non-stop at the breakfast table and never put the milk back in the fridge.

On the positive side, although stage theories may indeed offer a view of relationships as considerably more fixed, linear and predictable than they really are, they do offer a framework within which the complexity of real relationships can be explored. They are also useful in suggesting many testable hypotheses about the kinds of variables that may affect relationships at different times in their life cycle.

> 1 Draw your own flow diagrams to represent the different filters or stages in the models of Kerckhoff and Davis and of Murstein.
> 2 After you have drawn the framework, try to think of everyday examples that apply in each case (for example, in the 'stimulus' stage of Murstein's model, you may reject someone because they are too short, or go on to the next stage because someone has blue eyes and blond hair, characteristics which you like).
> 3 Draw a similar flow diagram for Levinger's ABCDE model, putting in the initial letters and words they stand for in each box and a very brief summary of what each stage comprises.

Review exercise

Summary

- *Stage theories* of relationships propose that relationships go through different stages in their formation, lifetime or dissolution. *Filter theories* are a type of stage theory concerned with the way in which we selectively filter out people in our search for a partner.
- *Kerckhoff and Davis' filter theory* proposes that during courtship we first select people on the basis of opinions and attitudes (usually similar ones), then on complementary personality traits.
- *Murstein's stimulus-value-role model theory* says that when we select an intimate partner, we first select on the basis of physical attributes (stimulus), then by attitudes and opinions (value) and finally on whether or not we both agree on roles within the partnership.
- *Levinger's stage theory model* proposes five possible stages in the course of close relationships (both intimate and friendly ones). These are A – acquaintance, B – buildup, C – continuation, D – deterioration, E – ending.
- There are several problems with stage theories, the main one being that they are too inflexible – not all relationships go through the same stages in the same order.

Further reading

(The theories covered in this chapter are not covered in any great depth in most textbooks, so the only recourse to further reading is to use the original journal articles.)

Kerckhoff, A.C. and Davis, K.E. (1962) Value consensus and need complementarity in mate selection, *American Sociological Review* 27 (3), 295–303.

Lippa, R.A. (1990) *Introduction to Social Psychology*, Wadsworth. Chapter 11 (p. 397) discusses stage models of attraction, particularly that of Murstein.

Murstein, B. I. (1970) Stimulus–value–role: a theory of marital choice, *Journal of Marriage and the Family*, 32, 465–481.

6

The dissolution of relationships

Erich Fromm warned that 'there is hardly any activity, any enterprise, which is started with such tremendous hopes and expectations and yet which fails so regularly as love' (1956, in Sternberg and Barnes, 1988, p. 38). As escalating divorce statistics in the Western world demonstrate so starkly, many romantic relationships come to an end, as of course do other types of partnership. For this reason, recent research on relationships has begun to change from its previous focus on relationship formation to factors involved in relationship breakdown.

To some extent all relationships are unique, and each breakdown has features that are distinct from those which occur in other dissolving relationships. Nevertheless, it is possible to outline characteristics which are common features of most, if not all, relationship breakdown. In this chapter we will first look at conflicts in relationships, then at two models concerned with breakdown, one that suggests the phases involved in relationship dissolution and the other documenting the diverse ways people respond when they are dissatisfied with a relationship.

Conflicts in relationships

We are all familiar with what it's like to have arguments and disagreements, and we have all experienced times when other people irritate us intensely. These situations are caused by interpersonal conflicts which can be said to exist when the actions of one person interfere with the actions of another (Peterson, 1983). Conflict is inevitable in interpersonal relationships and its likelihood increases as two people become more interdependent – thus the closer the relationship, the more potential there is for conflict.

Friends, neighbours, work colleagues, parents and children, married and cohabiting couples all have disagreements from time to time but most research has centred on conflicts experienced by heterosexual couples. This is probably because when people live together their lives are so intertwined that there are a great many opportunities for disagreement. Nevertheless it is a shame, considering how important friendships and family relationships are in many people's lives.

Sources of conflict are manifold: people will argue about almost anything. Disagreements about money, sex, jealousy and who does which household chores all create serious conflict in intimate relationships (Kurdek, 1994). The major potential causes of interpersonal conflicts have been classified by Braiker and Kelley (1979) into three main categories:

- Conflicts over *specific behaviours*: 'you never wipe your feet'; 'you didn't send me a birthday card'; 'you're late'
- Conflicts over *norms and roles*: 'you should support me in this'
- Conflicts over *personal dispositions*: 'you're lazy and inconsiderate'; 'you worry about the most unimportant things'; 'you're a spend-thrift'

Attributions of behaviour in intimate relationships

The way in which annoying and irritating behaviours are interpreted can make a significant difference to whether or not conflicts are successfully resolved. Suppose that in a partnership one person forgets to buy a loaf of bread on the way home. This can be interpreted as a minor incidental matter caused by certain circumstances such as having other things on your mind. It can alternatively be attributed to a far more serious, negative aspect of personality, for example, that the miscreant is selfish, inconsiderate and lazy. Likewise positive behaviours, such as a cuddle or a gift, can be attributed in a negative fashion (he or she is after something) or a positive one (he or she is very affectionate).

Bradbury and Fincham (1990) have investigated the types of **attributions** (causes of behaviour) made by happy and unhappy couples. They suggest that there are significant differences in the way miserable as opposed to happy couples see the causes of their partner's behaviour. In essence, unhappy couples tend to view their partner's behaviour in a very negative light, even when the behaviour is one they would normally like (such as saying their partner is looking nice), and this attitude, hardly surprisingly, maintains or increases the dissatisfaction in the relationship. Happy couples, in contrast, view their partner's behaviour in a positive light, even when they don't particularly like the behaviour, and this serves to enhance the relationship. Figure 1 illustrates the model.

In essence, unhappy couples see any undesirable behaviour as:

- characteristic of the person (internal)
- long-lasting (stable)
- as applying to other areas of the relationship (global).

In contrast, desirable behaviour is seen as:

- due to circumstances (external)
- atypical of that person (unstable)
- applying only to that particular circumstance (specific).

Happy couples respond in a completely contrasting way. They see undesirable behaviour as:

- situational (external)
- temporary (unstable)
- unlikely to apply to other areas of the relationship (specific).

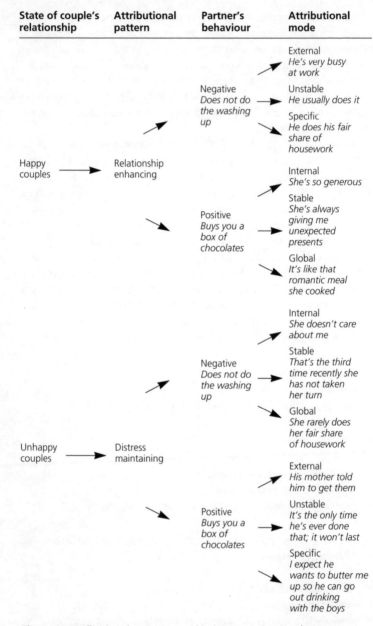

Figure 1 Attributional patterns used in happy and unhappy relationships

Positive actions are seen as:

- characteristic of that person (internal)
- liable to recur (stable)
- likely to apply in other areas of the relationship (global).

This type of research highlights the need when trying to resolve conflicts to think carefully not only about how others see the situation but whether our own attributions (assumptions about why a person has acted the way they have) are distress maintaining or relationship enhancing.

The positive side of conflicts

We generally think of conflicts as a negative component of inter-personal relationships but, as Duck (1992) and others have pointed out, conflicts can be positive when they provide the opportunity to clarify disagreements and negotiate roles in a relationship. Courting couples who sort out these controversial issues early in a relationship are less likely to have serious disagreements about them later on.

1   List sources of conflict and sources of power in one of your own relationships. With regard to conflicts, try to think of one for each of the categories mentioned earlier, i.e.:

- A conflict over a specific behaviour
- A conflict over norms and roles
- A conflict over personal disposition.

2   Think of an example (other than the ones used in the text) of a positive and an annoying behaviour. Using the attribution model of Bradbury and Fincham, think of how an unhappy and a happy couple might interpret both of these behaviours.

Progress exercise

Duck's model of relationship dissolution

Duck (1982) argues that relationship breakdown is not a single event but a *process* which occurs in a systematic manner over a period of

Dissolution States and Thresholds	Persons Concerns	Repair Focus
1. Breakdown: Dissatisfaction with relationship	Relationship process; emotional and/or physical satisfaction in relationship	Concerns over one's value as a partner; Relational process
Threshold: I can't stand this any more		
2. Intrapsychic Phase: Dissatisfaction with partner	Partner's 'faults and inadequacies'; alternative forms of relationship; relationships with alternative partners	Person's view of partner
Threshold: I'd be justified in withdrawing		
3. Dyadic Phase: Confrontation with partner	Reformulation of relationship: expression of conflict; clearing the air	Beliefs about optimal form of future relationship
Threshold: I mean it		
4. Social Phase: Publication of relationship distress	Gaining support and assistance from others; having own view of the problem ratified; obtaining intervention to rectify matters or end the relationship	Either: Hold partners together (Phase 1) Or: Save face
Threshold: It's now inevitable		
5. Grave-dressing Phase: Getting over it all and tidying up	Self-justification; marketing of one's own version of the break-up and its causes	

Figure 2 **A sketch of the main concerns at different phases of dissolution**
Source: Duck, 1984

time. He suggests that there are four different phases involved in a relationship dissolution and that each of these phases is initiated when a certain threshold of dissatisfaction is reached. Figure 2 illustrates the model.

The intrapsychic phase: focus on partner

This first, intrapsychic, phase begins when the threshold 'I can't stand it any more' is reached. One (or both) of the partners experiences dissatisfaction with how the relationship is going and spends a lot of time fretting about it. At this stage nothing is said to the partner, who may be oblivious to any problems. The distress either remains private or is shared with only one or two intimate friends who will not spill the beans to the partner.

The dyadic phase: focus on the relationship

When the threshold 'I'd be justified in withdrawing' is reached, the dyadic phase begins. If the relationship is not particularly formal, the end may be left implicit. Most of us are familiar with situations in which one party says something like 'I'll be in touch', 'I'll ring you', or the even vaguer 'See you around'. In relationships that involve marriage or cohabitation, the discontented party must face up to telling his or her partner. Discussions can then begin to repair or break up the relationship.

The social phase: facing the public consequences

If the negotiations are unsuccessful so that the threshold of 'I mean it' is reached, the dissolution moves into the social phase. The dissatisfaction and plans for breakup now become public, and each partner confides in others in an attempt to enlist support for their version of events. There is still a possibility that things can be patched up and in some cases the parties may seek outside help (an 'intervention team') to try to put their side of the story to the other partner. If, however, the relationship does come to an end, it is essential that each party makes public a version of events that doesn't make them look as if they have behaved badly. Both in this social phase and in the next, gossip is an important means of disseminating the justification of actions taken.

The grave-dressing phase: tidying up the accounts

The final, grave-dressing phase begins once the threshold of 'It's now inevitable' is reached. As Duck (1992) says, once the relationship is dead we have to bury it 'good and proper' – with a tombstone saying how it was born, what it was like, and why it died. We have to create an account of the relationship's history and, as it were, put that somewhere so that other people can see it and, we hope, accept it.

(p. 97)

One of the most important aspects of the grave-dressing (and the social) phase is that we leave the relationship without damaging our reputation. Duck points to the work of La Gaipa (1982) who says that once a relationship is over, we try to ensure that our 'social credit' is intact by taking little or no personal blame for the breakup. Either we blame conditions that existed before the start of the relationship, or external circumstances, or our partner, or any combination of these. Familiar types of comments made at this stage are: 'I really tried, but no matter what she says, I'm sure she had never really got over Gerry. I didn't stand a chance'; 'He was never at home, always in the pub while I was stuck in with the kids – that's no life'. The type of comment *not* made is: 'I'm basically a selfish pig. I never really gave a damn about him and once the novelty wore off, I fancied taking my chances in a new bed. I think monogamy is very overrated.' Such an ill-advised remark would, needless to say, seriously lower the amount of 'credit' that could be offered to a new relationship.

Commentary on Duck's model

Duck's model has some useful practical implications for the repair of relationships and has been used to develop a new model that looks at strategies whereby a relationship can be repaired (Duck, 1994). He suggests that in some phases, certain behaviours will be more effective than others in trying to put things right. For example, in the intrapsychic phase, repair should aim at re-establishing liking for the partner by keeping a record of their positive aspects rather than dwelling on the negative. In the social phase, individuals outside the relationship (the intervention team) need to decide whether to advise the parties to try and repair the damage or if it would be better for the relationship to end with as much face saving as possible.

Previous research (as discussed in earlier chapters) has concentrated on the formation of relationships. Although theories such as social exchange and equity theory can be used to explain why relationships break down and how they can be repaired, these applications are limited simply because such theories have been concerned with the very early stages of the relationship when things are often going relatively well. Duck's model does not make any attempt to provide reasons for relationship breakdown but, together with its practical applications, it does demonstrate how the processes of dissolution and repair of relationships are closely intertwined.

Rusbult and Zembrodt's model of responses to relationship dissatisfaction

Rusbult and Zembrodt (1983) proposed a model designed to classify the reactions of people when a relationship becomes unsatisfactory. It is quite a general model, in that it applies to all types of relationships, including dissatisfaction in employer–employee relationships (Rusbult *et al.*, 1988), but we will consider how it was originally applied to romantic relationships.

According to this model there are four main responses to relationship dissatisfaction, and these responses vary on two dimensions: *active* or *passive*, and *constructive* or *destructive*.

Figure 3 provides an illustration of this.

ACTIVE
take action

	EXIT leave the relationship	**VOICE** discuss problems
DESTRUCTIVE responses that weaken or end the relationship		**CONSTRUCTIVE** responses intended to repair/maintain the relationship
	NEGLECT pull back from relationship	**LOYALTY** wait for relationship to improve

PASSIVE
take no direct action

Figure 3 **Responses to dissatisfaction in relationships**
Source: Based on Rusbult and Zembrodt, 1983

- *Voice*: an active, constructive response. Someone who uses the voice reaction literally voices their concerns out loud, usually in an attempt to improve the situation. Tactics include suggesting compromise, seeking help or trying to change themselves, their partner or both.
- *Loyalty*: a passive, constructive response. Loyalty response is essentially a supportive one in which the individual passively but optimistically waits for things to improve. Attitudes such as 'I'll give it some time', 'I'm going to try to forgive and forget' fall into this category.
- *Neglect*: a passive, destructive response. The neglect response involves a refusal to deal with the problem, thus letting the situation deteriorate through lack of effort. People may refuse to discuss problems, spend less time with their partner and criticise them, often behind their back.
- *Exit*: an active, destructive response. An exit response involves getting out of the relationship altogether. Exit responses include moving out of the shared home and filing for divorce.

It is very important to note that in this model the dimension destructive/constructive refers to the effect *on the relationship* of a particular response. Neglect and exit responses are liable to destroy the relationship, whereas voice and loyalty are aimed at maintaining it. These terms are not intended as value judgements on the individuals involved. If a person who has been physically and mentally abused for many years chooses 'exit' as a response, this is likely to be a very constructive and personally helpful response *for the individual*, even though its effect on the relationship is destructive.

Commentary on Rusbult and Zembrodt's model

This model is not simply descriptive: much research has been conducted on the relationship between choice of response and the circumstances of the relationship. Some of the research findings reported by Rusbult *et al*. (1982) are as follows:

- Women are more likely than men to use *voice*.
- People who are well educated are more likely to use *voice*, while those with less education are more liable to respond by *loyalty* or *neglect*.

- If there are plenty of available alternatives, the response is likely to be active (*exit* or *voice*) rather than passive (*loyalty* or *neglect*).
- If the relationship has previously been very satisfactory, the investment is high and there are few suitable alternatives, the likely response is a constructive one (*voice* or *loyalty*).
- When the relationship has been very unsatisfactory, little has been invested in it and there are reasonable alternatives, the most likely response is *exit*.
- When relationship problems are considered to be relatively minor, and either there are few alternatives or there has been considerable investment (or both), the most popular response is *loyalty*.

The last three findings are those that would be predicted by social exchange theory and equity theory (see Chapter 4) and extend the ideas of these theories to show the different ways in which people react to problems in a relationship.

On the negative side, as Duck (1988) comments, although this model has generated much useful information concerning gender and demographic differences (differences between people from a variety of groups within society) in response to dissatisfaction, it does not tell us anything about the *process* of falling out and recuperating from disruption.

This model provides us with symptoms of dissatisfied relationships but it is not yet clear whether these modes of responding are also *causes* of the problems.

Concluding comments

Duck (1982), among others, points out that there are certain problems with researching relationship dissolution. Although it is possible to study relationships at a time when problems become apparent, this is not usually done for fear that it may alter the course of events and perhaps precipitate a breakdown that may not otherwise have occurred. Most breakdowns are therefore studied in retrospect (after the event), which means that what actually happened is not always accurately recorded. For this reason it is possible that the very earliest stages of dissatisfaction tend not to be reported (Duck, 1982).

The breakdown of a relationship is often a very distressing experience. Duck (1992), in a review of many studies, reports that, compared to others of similar age and sex, people in disrupted relationships suffer greater levels of depression and coronary heart disease and have lower levels of self-esteem. However, the tacit assumption that such experiences are always negative is now being challenged, and there is increasing recognition that leaving a relationship can be a very liberating experience. Now that relationship dissolution is neither unusual nor greatly stigmatised, breaking down and patching up are becoming a major focus of relationship research.

Review exercise

1 According to Bradbury and Fincham (1990), what type of *attributions* do happy couples make to undesirable behaviour? How does this differ from the attributions made by unhappy couples to the same type of behaviour?

2 Imagine that the relationship you have with one of your colleagues in your job is an unhappy one. Apply Rusbult and Zembrodt's model and think of a response that would correspond to each of the following: *voice, neglect, loyalty, exit.*

3 Match the phase to the threshold:

(a)	dyadic phase	(i)	It's now inevitable
(b)	grave-dressing phase	(ii)	I mean it
(c)	intrapsychic phase	(iii)	I'd be justified in withdrawing
(d)	social phase	(iv)	I can't stand it any more

4 Match the response to the two places on the dimensions:

(a)	voice	(i)	Active–destructive
(b)	loyalty	(ii)	Active–constructive
(c)	exit	(iii)	Passive–destructive
(d)	neglect	(iv)	Passive–constructive

Summary

- *Conflict* is inevitable in relationships and its likelihood increases as two people become more interdependent. The way in which annoying and irritating behaviours are *interpreted* can make a considerable difference to whether or not conflicts are successfully resolved. Bradbury and Fincham (1990) have produced a model describing how this applies to happy and unhappy marriages. Duck suggests that when conflicts are successfully negotiated, they can enhance understanding between people and improve a relationship.

- *Duck's model of relationship dissolution* proposes four phases in relationship breakdown. The intrapsychic phase is reached when one or both partners feels they can't stand it anymore. The dyadic phase is precipitated by the feeling that we are justified in leaving. The social phase involves making this justification public and perhaps seeking outside help to put things right. In the grave-digging phase the relationship is finally ended, with each partner making public a version of the breakdown that does not jeapordise their chances of developing a new relationship.

- *Rusbult and Zembrodt's model of relationship dissatisfaction* suggests that there are four kinds of behaviour that people use to deal with relationship dissatisfaction: voice, exit, loyalty and neglect.

Further reading

Duck, S. (1992) *Human Relationships* (2nd edn), London: Sage. Chapter 3 covers his theory in detail. It also discusses different ways of handling the breakup of relationships and how the model relates to 'putting it right'.

Lippa, R.A. (1990) *Introduction to Social Psychology*, CA: Wadsworth. Chapter 11 covers the Rusbult and Zembrodt model in a very accessible way.

McGhee, P.M. (1996) Make or break? The psychology of relationship dissatisfaction and breakdown, *Psychology Review* 2 (4), 27–30. This article looks at both of the models covered in this chapter (as well as others) and discusses methodologies involved in relationship breakdown. It also considers positive and negative aspects of breakdown and future developments.

7

Components and effects of relationships

Components of relationships: self-disclosure
Components of relationships: rules
Components of relationships: power
Health and happiness

We are all involved in relationships of one sort or another, and perhaps it is because of this that we are fascinated by what happens within them, especially with regard to sexual relationships. There are a very large number of aspects that can be investigated, and in this chapter we will take a brief look at some of these. We will begin by considering the processes by which people's knowledge of each other deepens, then at the unspoken rules that govern the way people behave towards one another and consider the distribution of power within relationships. Finally we will look at the effects of relationships on our health and happiness.

Components of relationships: self-disclosure

One of the most important processes in the formation of a close relationship is that of **self-disclosure**, the revealing of private and personal information about yourself that could not, as far as you are concerned, be acquired otherwise.

Self-disclosure is a *gradual* process: people do not usually reveal their innermost thoughts and feelings at a first encounter. It is also a *mutual* process: both parties exchange intimate facts and feelings to each other; if one holds back, the disclosures cease.

Altman and Taylor (1973) discuss this process of self-disclosure in their **social penetration theory**, so-called because it considers the ways in which, as relationships grow increasingly more intimate, they penetrate more and more deeply into the private, social and mental life of the self. The general trend as a relationship develops is for self-disclosures to become less superficial and more intimate; that is, they increase in *breadth* by covering more areas, and in *depth* by covering more and more sensitive and important topics.

Altman and Taylor describe the following changes that occur in the types of exchange as a relationship becomes more intimate. In the *orientation stage* we engage in a lot of 'small talk' and use non-controversial clichés ('it takes all sorts', 'practice makes perfect'). Then follows the *exploratory affective* stage in which we express personal attitudes ('I'm not keen on Christmas myself, it's a bit too commercialised now: OK for the kids though') but avoid intimate ones. In the early stages of self-disclosure we do not tell the whole truth and nothing but the truth: we provide limited and even false information about ourselves in order to give a favourable impression. Many interpersonal relationships never get beyond the exploratory affective exchanges, but those that do move on to the *affective stage* during which we now begin to discuss very personal and private matters, and this level of self-disclosure is accompanied by physical affection. Friends, especially female friends, may touch affectionately, lovers will kiss and touch intimately. Very close relationships will eventually reach the stage of *stable exchange* in which all personal feelings and possessions are shared and each can readily predict the feelings and behaviour of the other.

As mentioned above, the process of self-disclosure is a mutual one in which any exchanges made by one person must be matched by the other or the relationship will not deepen. This matching process is especially important in the early stages of a relationship, but later on strict reciprocity is not necessary, as the relationship is sufficiently well established not to require it.

The increase in intimacy is not necessarily a smooth and gradual one. Many relationships follow a more variable, cyclical pattern of self-disclosure (Altman *et al.*, 1981; Derlega *et al.*, 1993). Some pairs mutually self-disclose very quickly, then stop quite abruptly; others show a quick start and then a plateau, while others show a steady rise followed by a lull or a decline.

When relationships that were intimate begin to break down, self-disclosures often narrow to a very few acrimonious topic areas, but they are still deeply penetrating as partners bombard each other with hurtful insults and recriminations (Tolstedt and Stokes, 1984).

Commentary

There are well-documented gender differences in self-disclosure. Women disclose more than men, but the difference is not particularly large and depends on the sex of the person to whom the disclosures are being made; for example, men will disclose more to a woman than to another man. The greatest differences in self-disclosure, and they are considerable, are that women disclose far more to other women than men do to other men (Dindia and Allen, 1992). The stereotyped idea of pairs of men in pubs discussing football, cars and work while pairs of women mull over the most intimate aspects of their sex and family lives has a ring of truth to it, at least in white Western society. Gender differences in self-disclosure are, however, fairly complex and are discussed in more detail in Chapter 8.

The importance of self-disclosure in any relationship should not be underestimated. When we share intimate information about ourselves to others, we are showing that we trust them not to violate our confidences and that we are committed to the relationship. By such revelations, we are inviting them to make their own disclosures and thereby to enter into a close and mutually supportive relationship with us.

1   Try to remember the last time you met someone for the first time and got to know them (perhaps when you started college, or went into the sixth form at school). Did the conversations correspond to the sequence of disclosures outlined by Altman and Taylor? Next time you meet someone new, see if the initial chats correspond to the orientation stage.

Progress exercise

continued . . .

2 Why are hairdressers and publicans advised not to go beyond this stage with people whom they meet in the course of their work? What might happen if they did not adhere to the unwritten rule of never mentioning politics or religion?

Components of relationships: rules

Imagine the following situation. You have phoned a friend and asked her to meet you for a drink, but she declines, saying she's not feeling too well and perhaps you could meet another time. Later on that evening, you pass by a restaurant and see her enjoying a cosy meal with another friend. In this situation most of us would feel very hurt, and the friendship would be in jeopardy. Your friend has not played by the rules. She has lied to you. We may not consciously be aware of the rules that govern relationships, but we know when these rules have been broken.

Argyle and Henderson (1985) define rules as 'behaviour that most people think or believe should be performed, or should not be performed' (p. 37). Rules are developed so that people's goals in different relationships or situations can be attained. These rules provide a key to the skills needed to cope with relationships successfully and enable us to understand them better.

Argyle and Henderson (1985) have conducted extensive research into the rules people use in different types of relationships, and the section that follows is based on that research.

Types of rules

There are many different kinds of rules for relationships. Before reading further, take a look at Figure 4, which provides examples of rules from different relationships. Notice that there is even a set of rules for 'people you can't get on with'.

We can classify rules into four main categories:

1 *Rewardingness rules*: Social exchange theory (Chapter 4) tells us that we will only stay in a relationship if the rewards minus the costs are greater than we can get in alternative relationships, allowing for the cost of transfer. Some rules operate to keep

rewards and costs at an acceptable level and we would expect these to apply to all relationships. Rules of rewardingness may be 'you must be polite' and 'you should not cause embarrassment to others'.

2 *Intimacy rules*: Relationships vary greatly in the degree of intimacy they permit. Family and friends have completely different rules than do relationships with neighbours and workmates. Some rules of intimacy actually operate to keep intimacy low. Examples of rules of intimacy may be 'you do not kiss people at work' and 'always kiss your spouse goodbye before you leave for work'.

3 *Rules for coordination and avoiding difficulties*: These operate so that goals can be achieved with a minimum of problems. These rules, unlike those of rewardingness, are specific to each relationship. An example of such a rule as applied to a doctor–patient relationship may be 'always tell the doctor the truth'.

4 *Rules of behaviour with third parties*: Relationships do not simply consist of pairs of people, they also involve others. Rules of behaviour with third parties are necessary in order to control behaviour in relation to other people and they help to deal with problems of jealousy, keeping confidences and defending someone in their absence. Such rules may include 'you do not have sex with anyone other than your spouse' and 'if someone criticises your friend, you challenge them'.

Clustering of rules

Statistical analysis shows that relationships fall into a number of clusters, each cluster sharing similar rules. In Britain, one cluster contains spouse, siblings and close friends, another contains doctor, teacher and work superior. The relationships that form a cluster in one culture will not necessarily be clustered similarly in a different culture.

Cultural variation in rules

There is considerable variation in rules between different cultures; an example of which many people are aware is the difference in greeting between non-intimate people in Britain and France: a formal handshake in Britain and the more intimate cheek kissing in France.

Rules for friendship
Volunteer help in times of need
Seek to repay debts, favours and compliments
Show emotional support
Be tolerant of each other's friends

Rules for a dating relationship
Show mutual trust
Be punctual
Be faithful to one another
Touch the other person intentionally

Rules for marriage (both spouses)
Create a harmonious home atmosphere
Give birthday cards and presents
Inform the partner about one's personal schedule
Talk to partner about religion and politics

Rules for in-laws: both parents and children
Don't engage in sexual activity
Invite each other to family celebrations
Remember birthdays
Repay debts, favours or compliments

Rules for subordinates at work
Don't hesitate to question when orders are unclear
Put forward and defend own ideas
Be willing and cheerful
Be willing to take orders

Rules for two people who don't get on with each other
Should strive to be fair in relations with one another
Should not invite to dine in family celebrations
Should not feel free to take up as much of the other's time as one desires
Should not ignore the other person

Figure 4 Examples of rules of different relationships
Source: Examples taken from Argyle and Henderson (1985)

Cultural variations in rules can cause considerable misunderstanding, especially when an accepted rule in one culture is frowned upon or even illegal in another. For example, in some countries it is expected that people will help their relatives by giving them jobs, while in other cultures this kind of favouritism is deemed unethical.

Functions of rules

Rules serve two major functions in relationships:

1 They regulate behaviour to minimise potential sources of conflict that may disrupt the relationship. Such rules are referred to as 'regulating rules'.
2 They provide an exchange of rewards that motivate the individual to stay in the relationship. These rules are known as 'reward rules'.

Since different relationships have different goals, the rules obviously differ. For example, rules in work relationships (such as doctor–patient) are almost exclusively regulating rules. In contrast, friendship rules include many rules about exchange of rewards, and marriage involves many reward rules designed to maintain intimacy.

Components of relationships: power

Social power can be defined as the ability of a person to make demands on another and to have those demands met. Power is a very important influence in any relationship – in friendships, among co-workers, between family members and especially between lovers.

An obvious example of power in a relationship is that of a boss over a worker, although the worker also has some power in this relationship. Friendships may represent a more egalitarian (equal) relationship but each partner has power over the other – the power to influence decisions, the power to have advice taken seriously and without offence, the power to hurt another's feelings.

Power is based on the control of valuable resources. Different types of power are based on having different types of resources. French and Raven (1959) classify sources of social power into five main categories:

1 *Coercive power* stems from the ability to dispense punishment.
2 *Reward power* stems from the ability to dispense rewards.
3 *Legitimate power* depends on one person's acceptance of role obligations to follow instructions or advice.
4 *Referent* power stems from the desire to identify with or emulate someone.
5 *Expert power* depends on having superior knowledge and ability.

In any relationship there is unlikely to be only one type of power operating but one may predominate. For example, our friends have referent power over us because we identify with them and want them to like us. In an intimate relationship, power depends on several factors including:

- *Psychological dependency* of each partner on the relationship.
- *Social norms*, for example, sex role expectations (such as the belief that it is expected that a man will earn more than the woman and both will feel uncomfortable if that is not the case).
- *Personal resources* brought by each party to the relationship (attractiveness, income, skills and so on).

If, in a relationship, one partner is more committed and dependent than the other, this significantly influences the balance of power within that relationship. Waller and Hill (1951) advanced the **principle of least interest**, which states that the person who is less interested in continuing the relationship has greater power and therefore greater influence over what happens. You will recognise this easily from everyday experiences and observations. If Chris is deeply in love with Les, but Les is not particularly smitten with Chris, Les has considerably more power to dictate terms in the relationship than does Chris. Related to this aspect of power in a relationship is the number of alternatives available. Those who have many admirers have more power than those whose choice is limited.

Personal resources brought to a relationship also influence the balance of power: the greater the resources, the greater the power. Many women remain in marriages with which they are not happy because they fear the financial consequences of leaving.

Social norms also influence power relationships, and this is particularly relevant to male and female roles in intimate relationships. Men are physically stronger than women, so they have greater coercive power (the power to use physical force) should they choose to use it. Married men often have more resources (in terms of greater income and education), which means that wives tend to be more dependent on their husbands for security than vice versa and it is the men who usually have greater power to control money and other valuable commodities, so they have greater reward power. For all of these reasons, it is hardly surprising that most marriages are not egalitarian and that the power resides quite firmly with the man (Peplau and Gordon, 1983). On the other hand, as women gain resources in terms of better education, economic power and self-confidence, it is likely that the balance of power in relationships will change (Scanzoni, 1979).

The way in which power is distributed in a relationship affects the amount of satisfaction experienced by each partner. In a marriage there are a great many decisions to be made and power can therefore be exercised in many realms. Beach and Tesser (1993) found that marital satisfaction was higher when each member of a couple had the power to make decisions about things that mattered to that individual, for example, 'you can choose the car if I can decide where we go on holiday'.

As you would expect, if one person in a relationship wields so much power that they make nearly all the choices, the person who rarely gets their own way is unlikely to be content. Ultimately, relationships based on an imbalance of power are usually unsatisfactory to both partners and may either change towards a more equal balance of power or they may end.

Health and happiness

Research indicates that interpersonal relationships are good for us. Campell (1981) found that, at least among Americans, social relationships are a more important source of well-being than income, social status or education. One of the most positive events in life is gaining a relationship or improving an existing one; it leads to a better quality of life and a more pleasant general outlook (Reitch and Zautra, 1981). In contrast, the loss of a relationship can be one of the worst and most distressing experiences.

Although research indicates that most types of relationships, including those with family and friends, have an effect on both our happiness and health, most research has focused on the limited area of the effect of marriage on health. This is probably because statistics on marriage, divorce and health (especially mortality) are relatively easy to obtain, whereas data on the prevalence and strength of other relationships and measures of happiness are much more nebulous. Nevertheless, the balance is beginning to be redressed.

Effects on physical health

As long ago as 1851, and in many studies since, statistics have indicated that married people live longer than those who are unmarried (Farr, 1975; Hu and Goldman, 1990). The widowed and divorced are more susceptible to a range of illnesses than either the single or the married (Bloom *et al.*, 1978). They make more visits to the doctor and take more days off sick than their married and single counterparts. For both men and women, the healthiest are the married, followed by the single, then the widowed. Those who are separated or divorced are the least healthy (Cramer, 1995).

The obvious conclusion from this data is that marriage serves to protect our health, but since the association between length of life and marriage is a *correlation*, we cannot assume a cause-and-effect relationship on this alone. After all, it is quite possible that the healthy, especially the mentally healthy, are more likely to be chosen as marriage partners. In essence, we cannot be sure whether it is *selection procedure* or the *protection of marriage* or a third overriding factor (such as being rich, which makes you more healthy and more eligible) which contributes to the increased longevity of married people. Hu and Goldman's research gives us a clue to which is more important. As well as showing that married people live longer than those who have never married, it also showed that divorced and widowed individuals (who have by definition been chosen as marriage partners) on average die at an earlier age than married people. This suggests that marriage does offer some protection to health.

Nevertheless, we cannot entirely rule out the possibility that the unhealthy are less likely to seek out and find partners in the first place (Mastekassa, 1992). Neither can we dismiss prosperity as a third factor controlling both better health and better marriage prospects. As Durkin (1995) remarks, rich people are not only very likely to get married because they are a very attractive proposition, but 'the lovely and the loaded tend to live well, and are less exposed to malnutrition, hazardous environments, depression, and other health threats associated with lower social status' (p. 611).

With regard to other relationships, physical health is better for the employed than for the unemployed who have lost relationships with work colleagues (although factors other than relationship loss may be implicated here), and for those with children compared with the childless (Warr, 1983).

In a longitudinal study, Berkman and Syme (1979) obtained satisfaction ratings of the social support provided by marriage, by close friends and family, by the church and by various organisations in over 4,700 adults aged between 30 and 69. Nine years later they looked at how many had died. Those with good social support in all areas, but especially that provided by marriage and by friends and family, were least likely to have died. One criticism of this study is that it used self-rating scales for initial health assessment. Nevertheless, many other studies, including some that have used more objective measures, have revealed similar findings.

Effects on mental health

Close, harmonious relationships are particularly important for good mental health but discordant ones can cause serious problems. The divorced and separated are more likely than the married to commit suicide, suffer from depression and alcoholism and receive treatment for psychiatric disorders, and the effect for men is considerably greater than for women (Gove, 1979).

Brown and Harris (1978) reported that women experiencing considerable stress were much less likely to be depressed if they had a supportive spouse with whom to share their problems than if they had no such social support. However, Fincham (1997), after surveying a hundred couples, concluded that although marriage is beneficial to the mental health of men, it has the opposite effect in women who are very often depressed within their marriages. These very different findings may reflect the fact that women, like men, benefit from a supportive relationship but, once things start to go wrong and there is marital disharmony, women become susceptible to depression. In men, discord within the marriage (as opposed to separation or divorce) does not have the same effect. Once the marriage breaks down and the couple separate, it is men who suffer more, probably because they have a smaller social network from which to gain support. In essence then, women tend to suffer more *within* marriage if it is a discordant one, whereas men suffer more *after* the marriage has ended.

Again, we must bear in mind that cause–effect may not be obvious. It is possible that increases in conditions such as depression and alcoholism are not caused by divorce but are the reason for it, although the divorce itself may then cause an increase in the severity of these conditions.

93

Effects on happiness

Happiness, as mentioned earlier, is not an easy concept to measure and is usually done by means of rating scales.

In terms of short-term benefits (which have a long-term cumulative effect), life tends to be more enjoyable when we are with friends. This may be because when we are with friends we engage in enjoyable activities and have fun. Larson (1990) electronically tagged participants who were asked when 'beeped' at random intervals to report how happy they felt and who they were with at the time. On the whole, people were most happy when with their friends, followed by being with family, and were least happy when alone.

Evidence suggests that married people are happier than unmarried individuals. Although the difference is not great, married people at all ages report higher levels of satisfaction than do single people (Campell, 1981).

Within marriage, there are various models which attempt to show the course of satisfaction. Pineo (1961) suggests that after the first flush of passion during courtship and the very early years, there is a steady decline in happiness thereafter. However, Burr (1970) proposes a curvilinear relationship of satisfaction over time. Typically, couples are happiest in the early years before children, least satisfied in the years after childbirth, and return to a higher level of satisfaction in later years, although this level never quite returns to that of the 'honeymoon' years. Research strongly supports the idea, suggested by both models, that there is a decline in happiness in the early years of marriage. Whether or not satisfaction levels remain at this lower level or increase again is a matter of controversy. It is unlikely, anyway, that one pattern of marital satisfaction will adequately account for all marriages and both models probably apply; the debatable point is which one is the more typical course.

Fincham (1997) points out that simply measuring 'marital satisfaction' as a single entity is inadequate to express differences and similarities in happiness between married couples. He asks us to consider two very different couples: one couple simply 'get along' with no great highs or lows in their relationship; the other couple have violent arguments and fights but also have good laughs and great sex. On a unidimensional scale of marital satisfaction they may both emerge as 'moderate', but obviously the two relationships are very different. Fincham therefore suggests that we need to measure both positive and negative qualities in order to obtain a better picture. On this basis, the first couple mentioned above would score low on both positive and negative dimensions (a so-called *indifferent* relationship) while the second couple would score high on both (an *ambivalent* relationship). This reconceptualising of marital quality may eventually lead to a more sophisticated understanding of what constitutes happiness within a marital relationship.

Effects of loss of a relationship

The loss of an important relationship is one of the most stressful events in life and has a serious effect on both our physical and mental health. Events like the death of a close family member or friend are one of the main causes of depression. The death rate in men increases 40 per cent in the six months after a wife's death (sometimes due to suicide) but falls rapidly after that. For women, the effect is greatest in the second or third year after a husband's death (Gibson, 1992).

The effects of divorce are not quite the same for men and women. Although it is likely to increase depression in men, women often become less depressed once a stressful relationship is terminated, since they are likely to seek out and obtain a great deal of social support from other relationships, namely from family and friends.

Gender differences in the benefits of relationships

Having looked at some of the differential effects of marriage on the mental health of men and women, we will now consider other effects. Many studies show that, overall, marriage is more beneficial to husbands than it is to wives. Women provide more support than men do: they are more affectionate, appreciative, encouraging and more inclined to share intimacy (Argyle and Henderson, 1985). Divorce or loss of a spouse through death has a more damaging effect on men than it does on women.

Why is this? Remember that it is *psychological intimacy* and not marriage itself that produces benefits, and many people, particularly women, find social support and intimacy in close friendships and non-marital romantic relationships. Marriage is generally inequitable, with men having more power within it, and they also have interesting jobs, both of which make positive contributions to health and happiness. Wives, on the other hand, receive less emotional support from their husbands than vice versa and do the vast majority of boring household tasks which provide little satisfaction (Argyle and Henderson, 1985).

An article by Cook (1997) entitled 'Is marriage driving women mad?' considers the relative benefits of marriage for men and women in light of recent research on marriage breakdown (see further reading at the end of this chapter).

Reasons why social support affects health and happiness

The social support provided by relationships shows most powerfully during times of stress, since it can greatly ameliorate its effects. When something horrible happens or we feel we can't cope, we turn to our family and friends for help and support.

The positive effect this has may be a *direct effect*, because people look after each other in a physical way, for example, by cooking meals, doing the shopping and ensuring that medicine is taken. Social networks, such as self-help groups for the seriously ill, may also provide information that is of practical help.

Social support may also have an *indirect effect* in that it helps us cope more effectively with stress. There is a great deal of support for the **buffer effect of social support**; that is, people who feel supported are less affected by stressful events. Cohen and Hoberman (1982) found that, of people who felt their life to be very stressful, those who received little social support suffered more symptoms such as headaches, weight loss and sleep disturbances than those who perceived themselves as having high support.

Nuckolls *et al.* (1972) compared complication rates in pregnant women who were experiencing different levels of stress. They found that 91 per cent of women with high stress and low social support suffered complications, compared to 33 per cent who also suffered high stress but had high levels of social support.

Why does social support affect physical health? One reason may be its affect on the immune system. Goleman (1990) found that seriously ill people who joined support groups had more effective immune systems and tended to live longer than those without such support.

An analysis of many studies shows that the beneficial effects of social support are greatest when given to women and provided by family and friends. It is difficult to determine the relative contribution of direct benefits versus the indirect benefits of a companionate relationship but both are obviously important.

The negative effects of relationships

So far in this section we have looked at the positive effects of having relationships and the negative effects of ending close ones. We must not, however, ignore the fact that relationships themselves can be a source of stress, and when this stress outweighs the benefits of social support the overall effect is a negative one. As mentioned earlier, there is some evidence that loss of a relationship through divorce or separation can sometimes improve happiness, especially in women. For example, divorce and single parenthood can make a mother more confident and a child feel more loved (Woolett, quoted in Cooper, 1996).

On the whole, then, it is fair to conclude that relationships are generally good for our health and happiness but we need to acknowledge that they can also be a source of stress which, when ended, can improve our well-being.

---

1 Describe the four *types* of rules that exist for any relationship.
2 With regard to French and Raven's five categories of social power, choose three different types of relationship (for example, worker–employee) and say what types of power are likely to be wielded by each of the partners.
3 Outline the ways in which the *social support* offered by a relationship may have a positive effect on health.
4 Why does marriage appear to be more beneficial to men than to women?

Review exercise

Summary

- *Self-disclosure* involves revealing private and personal information about yourself to another person. It is one of the most important components of a relationship. *Social penetration theory* (Altman and Taylor, 1973) states that self-disclosure becomes more intimate and covers more areas of life (it increases in depth and breadth) as a relationship progresses. There are individual differences and gender differences in self-disclosure.

- *Rules* of relationships are behaviours that most people think or believe should or should not be performed. There are four main categories of rules: rewardingness rules, intimacy rules, rules for coordination and avoiding difficulties; and rules of behaviour with third parties. There is considerable variation in rules between cultures and this can cause misunderstanding, especially when a rule that is accepted in one culture is frowned upon in another.
- *Power* is a very important influence in any relationship. In an intimate relationship, power depends on psychological dependency, social norms and personal resources. The *principle of least interest* states that the person who is less interested in continuing a relationship has greater power and therefore greater influence over what happens. The way power is distributed in a relationship affects the amount of satisfaction experienced by each partner.
- *Health and happiness* can be affected by relationships. Most research in this area has concentrated on marriage. In general, married people tend to be happier and healthier than unmarried people. Of particular importance seems to be the role of social support in improving health and aiding recovery from illness. Social support for men comes largely from marriage, whereas women have a wider network of social support. Although relationships are generally good for you, they can also be a source of stress.

Further reading

Argyle, M. and Henderson, M. (1985) *The Anatomy of Relationships*, Harmondsworth: Penguin. Chapter 2 looks in detail at the effects of relationships.

Cochrane, R. (1996) Marriage and madness, *Psychology Review* 3 (1), 2–5. This article considers the various reasons why those who are married suffer fewer mental health problems than the unmarried.

Cook, E. (1997) Is marriage driving women mad?, *Independent on Sunday*, 10 August. This considers new research by Fincham. It uses everyday examples of relationships to discuss and interpret his findings.

Cramer, D. (1995) Personal relationships, *The Psychologist* 8 (2) (February). This edition of *The Psychologist* is mentioned at the end of several chapters since it is a special edition on relationships and is therefore well worth reading. This particular article considers the effects of relationships, particularly on health, and the problems of trying to establish cause and effect.

Fincham, F.D. (1997) Understanding marriage: from fish scales to milliseconds, *The Psychologist* 10 (12) (December). This article looks in detail at what we mean by marital satisfaction and at more sophisticated ways of assessing it.

8

Individual, social and cultural variations in relationships

- Homosexual relationships
- Gender differences in same-sex friendships
- Cross-cultural differences in heterosexual relationships

There is obviously a huge variety in the nature of relationships both within and between social classes and cultures. In this chapter, we take a snapshot view of just three from this vast array: homosexual relationships, same-sex friendships, and long-term heterosexual relationships in different cultures.

Homosexual relationships

The columnist Anna Quindlen (1992) remarked: 'children learn that the world is composed exclusively of love and sex between men and women.' A glance through the section on interpersonal relationships in most textbooks or even a reading of whole books on the subject could easily lead one to a similar conclusion. Homosexual relationships simply aren't there. When any reference is made to them, it is often a one-sentence cursory dismissal, assuring the reader that in most respects, there is little difference between a homosexual and a heterosexual relationship or, if differences are acknowledged, just saying that they are different without further specification. Such over-simplification conveys the assumption that we may legitimately use heterosexuality as the standard by which to compare all romantic relationships. As Huston and Schwartz (1995, p. 90) comment:

> To apply models derived from and appropriate for heterosexuals to homosexual relationships not only leads to questionable conclusions but also obscures a wealth of information about ways couples organise and conduct their relationships.

Relationships do not exist in isolation – they exist in a social context. Even though today's British society may be more liberal than the time – not so long ago – when homosexuality was illegal and people practising it were considered to be mentally ill (pathologised), the social context for homosexuals is still vastly different from that of heterosexuals. Heterosexuality is assumed, admired, celebrated (as on a wedding day) and economically supported. It is also very visible. People wear engagement and wedding rings, they have pictures of their family on their desks at work. On Monday mornings, they chat about what they and their partner have done over the weekend. Take a very ordinary scenario: an 18-year-old arrives at school or work one morning, a twinkle in the eye, full of the joys of spring, bursting to tell his or her friends that last night he or she met someone gorgeous (mentioning a member of the opposite sex) with whom they have a date the following Saturday night. Everyone is pleased for them and it is taken for granted that their joy, pleasure and pride can be shared. Can you imagine an 18-year-old gay man or lesbian making the same joyful announcement? I think not. A multitude of everyday minor celebrations of romantic attachments which heterosexuals take for granted are denied to homosexuals. As Kitzsinger and Coyle (1995) comment, you won't find gay and lesbian Valentine cards in the local newsagent.

Limitations to research

One of the greatest barriers to an understanding of homosexual relationships is the difficulty of obtaining a representative sample (Huston and Schwartz, 1995). There are several reasons for this. Many homosexuals choose not be open about their sexuality (not to 'come out'), especially those who fear it may have an adverse effect on child custody arrangements or employment prospects. Many older, more conservative homosexual couples are understandably reluctant to discuss their private lives. Non-cohabiting couples, who probably constitute a large percentage of the homosexual community, are difficult to find, as are homosexuals living in isolated and small communities. For these reasons, any research findings provide only a partial and limited view of gay and lesbian relationships – young, urban and extrovert. Bearing in mind these reservations, let us now consider some of these findings.

Similarities

Let us first consider some basic similarities between homosexual and heterosexual relationships. Homosexual relationships, like hetero-sexual ones, tend to last longer if the couple share similar attitudes and interests and have a similar level of commitment. The most satisfying relationships are those with high rewards, low costs and few alter-natives, as predicted by social exchange theory (discussed in Chapter 4). Like their heterosexual counterparts, many lesbians and gay men want to commit early and monogamously (McWhirter and Mattison, 1984).

Differences

Let us now move on to the many differences caused by the distinct social features of a homosexual relationship.

Stress

Having to tolerate homophobia (the intense dislike of homosexuals) which ranges from insults to property damage to life-threatening situations can take its toll on the peace of mind of lesbians and gay men and put strain on the relationship. Added stress can accrue if the couple cannot agree on the extent to which they should be 'out'. When relationships are experiencing problems, it is often difficult for gay men and lesbians to obtain support to help heal the rift. Relatives may be pleased that there are problems and encourage a relation-ship split. While troubled heterosexual couples can expect sympathy, counselling and encouragement in resolving relationship problems, homosexual couples receive little social support either during difficult times or after the relationship has ended (Becker, 1988).

Power

Unlike heterosexual females who seem to take for granted their relative lack of power compared to their male partner, lesbians put considerable value on an equitable (equal) balance of power in their intimate relationships. Although equality is not always achieved, at least the partners concede this and tend to view it as temporary and a goal to work towards. One of the reasons why men have such control in heterosexual relationships is because they have greater earning power. Research indicates that in lesbian relationships there is no connection between amount of earned income and power (Blumstein and Schwartz, 1983). In homosexual relationships the allocation of duties, especially household chores, is not taken for granted as in most heterosexual relationships, but is likely to be negotiated. As a result, power struggles are less frequent and dramatic in homosexual relationships as they are in heterosexual ones and underlying resentments about inequality do not have the same opportunity to fester (Peplau *et al.*, 1978).

Cohabitation

Cohabitation is less common among homosexuals than it is among heterosexuals (Harry, 1983). The reasons for this are complex, and include both practical and ideological considerations. On the practical side, cohabitation makes the relationship more visible which can be problematic, especially if ex-partners wish to use it as a lever in custody and access battles for children. In terms of ideology, there are several arguments. Firstly, homosexuals who have previously been in a heterosexual cohabiting relationship may not want to replicate a way of living they previously found unsatisfactory. Secondly, lesbians, as mentioned above, value autonomy and independence and may not feel that this is compatible with living in a shared household. Thirdly, and perhaps most importantly of all, homosexuals may reject the view held by a predominantly heterosexual society that, in order to be committed, couples need to live together and be economically interdependent. Whereas this may be of practical value to married couples with children, homosexuals are more likely to feel that you do not have to live together in order to be emotionally intimate and highly committed and indeed, on occasions, cohabitation may make this more difficult to achieve.

Sexual activity

One aspect of gay relationships that attracts much attention and implicit disfavour is the degree to which they are non-monogamous. Statistics indicate that within ten years of the onset of a committed relationship, 94 per cent of gay men and 43 per cent of lesbians, as compared to 30 per cent of married men and 22 per cent of married women, report having had sex outside the relationship (Blumstein and Schwartz, 1983). Based on a heterosexual yardstick, many researchers assume that the relatively high rate of non-monogamy must put a strain on gay male and lesbian relationships. However, there is a very significant difference in this respect between homosexual and heterosexual relationships. In the latter, sex outside the couple's relationship is unacceptable and, though quite frequent, is furtive, secretive and such a breach of trust that it is liable, if discovered, to signal the end of the relationship. In contrast, sexual activity outside a gay male or lesbian relationship is usually subject to negotiation of the relationship rules and is therefore far more honest and less likely to jeopardise it (Nichols, 1990).

In conclusion, we need to be aware that homosexuals are attempting to build relationships in a completely different social context from that of heterosexuals. Heterosexuality is sanctioned by the church and state and is celebrated in all walks of life. Homosexuality is ignored, condemned and penalised. As Kitzinger and Coyle (1995) emphasise, we must resist the temptation unthinkingly to apply heterosexual models to homosexual couplings, in which concepts of power and relationship success (to name just two) may have very different meanings. When comparing relationships that have institutional recognition with those that do not, we must take account of this before we can hope to have any appreciation of them. A deeper understanding of homosexual relationships and the ways in which they are affected by gender, power and social structures can provide an insight into ways in which society influences *all* our private relationships.

> Via the media, we are inundated by role models of heterosexuality (both in real life and fiction) that make us feel fine about our desire to be in such a relationship. You could probably think of half a dozen news stories and a similar number of films on current release that are concerned with a man and woman falling in love or breaking up and so on. Try to think of some role models that apply to homosexuals in this way.

Progress exercise

Gender differences in same-sex friendships

From an early age and throughout life there are significant sex differences in styles of friendships. The main gender difference in such friendships is neatly expressed by Wright (1982) as 'side-by-side' for male–male as opposed to 'face-to-face' for female–female. More formally, the differences have been labelled **instrumental** versus **expressive**. Instrumental friendships are those based on a sharing of activities; expressive friendships are those based on the sharing of emotions.

Childhood friendships

Sex segregation in friendship starts early. At around age 3 or 4, children show a preference for same-sex peers with whom to play and by age 9 or 10, as many of us will recall from our own childhood, it is an insult to suggest that a boy likes a girl.

In the school playground boys are inclined to play in large mixed-age groups, while girls are more often in smaller groups or same-sex pairs. Boys tend to play competitive team games that involve skills of cooperation, competition and leadership, whereas the activities enjoyed by girls tend to emphasise intimacy and exclusiveness (Lever, 1978). Differences have also been demonstrated in laboratory studies. If pairs of preschool boys who are strangers to each other are invited to play a game together, they simply get on with it. Pairs of similar aged girls, on the other hand, spend time getting to know each other and chatting about themselves (Shaver and Buhrmester, 1983).

The emphasis placed by girls on intimacy and self-disclosure goes hand in hand with the need for loyalty. In adolescence in particular, people who are intimate risk being humiliated if a disloyal friend reveals their most intimate desires and feelings to others. Because intimacy is essential in female friendships, girls are more likely than boys to be concerned about faithfulness and to worry about rejection by their friends (Buhrmester and Furman, 1987).

Our knowledge of the roots of the differences in same-sex childhood friendship is still in its infancy. As Bee (1992) comments, 'These are subtle but profound differences and we still know little about how they arise in earliest childhood and why they diverge so persistently. But this is obviously an important area for future research' (p. 446).

Adult friendships

With regard to adults, the patterns are essentially the same as those begun in childhood. Unger and Crawford (1992) reviewed several studies which showed that, compared to men's friendships, those between women tended to be more intimate, more intense and generally more important to the people involved. Several theorists suggest that women use friendship as a means to confide in each other. For women, getting together with friends often takes the form of asking them over for coffee to discuss personal matters. In contrast, men tend to choose friends from people with whom they share a mutual interest, so that they can enjoy joint activities such as fishing, watching football or playing a game of badminton (Sherrod, 1989).

Hayduk (1983) points out that men's competitiveness is inconsistent with sharing confidences, which may be a reason for their reluctance to do so. Interestingly, Rawlins (1992) suggests that, although competition is often central to the joint activities undertaken within male friendships, the *social interaction* in which they engage as part of these activities is often more important than winning or losing. It is almost as if men need an excuse to interact with each other, and this excuse is a joint activity which is enjoyable in itself but not the sole purpose of its existence.

Summary of same-sex differences in friendship

So far, we have said that compared to male–male friendships, female–female friendships are more confiding, more intimate and more emotionally expressive (Nardi and Sherrod, 1994). In male–male friendships there is more aggressive interaction, and discussion centres around shared interests and practical issues rather than self-disclosure and emotional expression (Sapadin, 1988). Compared to men, women have much more experience with intimate sharing from early childhood and are more comfortable with expressing vulnerability.

Why do these differences exist?

Reis *et al.* (1985) believe that these differences are not due to men's inability to be intimate; no differences between men and women are evident in their social skills. When requested by researchers to join in intimate conversations, men are quite as capable of doing this as are women and they are also able to judge from video fragments the different degrees of intimacy in a relationship. Reis *et al.* conclude that, should they so choose, men can have just as intimate interactions as women – but they prefer not to.

Socio-evolutionary theory argues that there are sound reasons why evolution favours the selection of 'instrumental' relationships between men and 'emotionally expressive' relationships between women. Based on work with chimpanzees, De Waal (1983) suggests that, in order to survive, it was necessary for males to undertake joint activities so that they could collaborate in hunting and fighting. Females, on the other hand, needed to be able to establish a supportive, nurturing network aimed at caring for the infants. This theory is largely speculative and overlooks the role of socialisation in favour of biology. In the main, studies suggest that both are important. The family, school and media all appear to play an important part in shaping behaviour, but some fundamental differences between men and women appear to persist despite different social and cultural influences. Since girls and boys are so differently socialised virtually from birth, it is impossible to disentangle the influence of biology from that of learning.

However . . .

Traditionally, researchers have drawn our attention to the differences rather than the similarities in male and female same-sex friendships. However, Duck and Wright (1993) contend that these differences may have been somewhat exaggerated. They have reanalysed earlier research findings and suggest that although women and men differ on a number of variables, the differences did not correspond to an instrumental versus expressive dichotomy. For example, when asked to give the reasons why they arranged to meet their friends, both men and women reported that they met most often just to talk, less often to engage in mutual activities and least often to deal with a relationship issue. Expressive and instrumental characteristics were about equally prominent aspects of a strong friendship for both men and women. Duck and Wright contend that both men and women are caring, supportive and encouraging in their relationships, but women are likely to express these feelings more openly. According to these researchers, just because, compared to women, men do not engage in such explicit displays of affection and personal disclosure does not mean that their friendships are any less emotional.

Consider your own same-sex friendships and make a list of the types of activities you share with these friends and the types of conversations you have with them. Go into some detail: for example, do you discuss your own personal experiences and attitudes or just talk about things in a general way? Does it depend on the topic area? Are there any taboo subjects? (For example, if you or one of your friends has suffered a bereavement, do you talk about it or is the subject avoided?)

If you can, compare your responses with those of at least one (preferably more) same-sex friendship of the opposite sex.

Progress exercise

Cross-cultural differences in heterosexual relationships

Much of the cross-cultural research in social psychology is based on a difference first outlined by Hofstede (1984) between **individualistic** and **collectivist** cultures. The major differences between such societies can be conveniently summarised as follows. Individualistic cultures, which include most Western nations, place the major emphasis on:

- self-interest and the interest of one's immediate family;
- personal autonomy (making your own decisions);
- individual initiative, individual achievement and independence.

Collectivist societies, which include most Eastern nations, place the major emphasis on:

- loyalty to the group that in turn looks after the interest of its members;
- interdependence;
- the belief that group decisions are more important than individual ones.

In collectivist cultures, people develop an emotional dependence on the group and believe that the needs and interests of others are paramount.

This divide is rather simplistic; for example, Mediterranean rural societies of Greece and Italy are collectivist within the family but individualistic outside it. Nevertheless, this distinction between cultures is helpful in looking at cultural differences in interpersonal relationships. Triandis *et al.* (1990) believe that the individualistic–collectivist dimension is one of the most important sources of cultural influences on social behaviour. We will consider the influence of this distinction on various aspects of heterosexual relationships.

Choosing a partner

Collectivist cultures usually adopt the practice of *arranged marriage* whereas in Western cultures individuals choose their own partners. This reflects one major variation in these different cultures: the extent to which individual *choice* plays a part in the formation of romantic heterosexual relationships, particularly marriage.

It is important to acknowledge that even in cultures in which marriages are arranged, most people have some choice in their eventual spouse, and even in Western societies choices are heavily influenced by families. That said, it is fair to say that the individualistic cultures put far more emphasis on individual choice in a partner than do collectivist societies. Since many readers will have an exclusively Western view of arranged marriages, let us take a look at the comments of a writer who, twenty-two years ago, when he considered himself to be a 'typical sixties London kid', went to Pakistan for an arranged marriage. Strongly supporting the practice, he debunks a common misconception:

> One of the first things that one has to appreciate about arranged marriages is that they have nothing to do with force. Forced marriages are just that – forced. They are common in tribal parts of India, Pakistan and Bangladesh and, in Britain, among sub-continental people from this background . . . they have little to do with arranged marriages. Arranged marriages are on a different plane: they involve negotiations between mutually consenting, concerned and caring people and are a great source of happiness – both before and after the event of marriage.
>
> (Sardar, 1999, p. 16)

Another cultural difference is the role of *romantic love* as a basis for choosing a marriage partner. In individualistic cultures, such as the USA and Britain, romantic love is seen as a very important pre-requisite to marriage, whereas collectivist cultures base choice of marriage partner on factors such as occupation and status. If people in collectivist cultures chose their own partners regardless of practical considerations, this would be disruptive to the functioning of the group and pose a threat to the coherence of a such a culture.

Some theorists suggest that romantic love as the basis for marriage (not in itself) is a relatively recent Western idea and that even in Europe it was not until the eighteenth century that it was entertained as a consideration where marriage was concerned (Hsu, 1971; Murstein, 1974). This does not mean that love plays no part in arranged marriages however. There is evidence that people in such marriages can eventually be more 'in love' than those who have made their own choices based on romantic love (see the paper by Gupta and Singh (1982), discussed in detail in Chapter 9).

In cultures where marriages are not arranged but are heavily influenced by parents (such as orthodox Jews), romantic love is again irrelevant if it would involve marriage outside the religious or ethnic group. In other words, in these cultures, romantic love is taken seriously only as long as it is directed towards a member of one's own group.

No amount of academic reading can make us appreciate some cross-cultural differences: it is necessary to have discussions with members of different cultures in order to appreciate an alternative viewpoint. There is a lot of misunderstanding about the nature of 'arranged marriages'. Whatever your background, try to find at least one person (preferably more) from a different background with regard to how choice of marriage partner is made and discuss in detail the basis of choice of lifetime partner and the pros and cons of the different types of practices.

Progress exercise

Assessing marital happiness

Another cross-cultural variation in interpersonal relationships is that *psychological intimacy* is more likely to be used as the basis on which to judge marital happiness and personal satisfaction in individualistic societies than in collectivist societies. In the US, people view marriage as providing the opportunity to experience personal growth through the relationship and thereby achieve self-fulfilment (Dion and Dion, 1993). This can result in very unrealistic expectations and a lack of appreciation of how difficult marriage can be – a rather naïve belief that 'love conquers all' (Heine and Lehman, 1995).

Dion and Dion (1993) argue that some aspects of being socialised in an individualistic society make it very difficult to sustain a satisfactory marriage. Western culture, with its emphasis on the importance of independence, personal control and autonomy, makes it very difficult to maintain intimacy even though this is seen as the major goal of a successful marriage. Dion and Dion suggest that this may account for the high divorce rate in the US and Canada. In contrast, collectivist societies place great value on dependency on others and this is therefore a highly valued aspect of close relationships.

Types of relationships studied

Before leaving the topic of cross-cultural relationships, it is worth taking note of the comments made in Chapter 1 about the kinds of relationships that Western psychologists tend to study. In this chapter and in many of the previous ones, the focus has been on romantic relationships and friendship, reflecting the major topics researched in the area of interpersonal relationships. The emphasis is very firmly on first-time acquaintances, close personal friendships and intimate partnerships because these are considered to be the most important relationships in Western culture, with relatively little attention paid to kinship and community relations. As Moghaddam *et al*. (1993) comment, 'The topic of interpersonal relationships provides an excellent example of how research topics reflect the characteristics of the societies from which they emerge' (p. 94). The balance is beginning to be redressed; for example, there is a growing recognition that in individualistic as well as collectivist cultures, kinship often provides our most important and intimate relationships (Argyle and Henderson, 1985), but we certainly have a long way to go. A more thorough cross-cultural perspective on interpersonal relationships would contribute greatly to a sensitive understanding of the nature and importance of such relationships both within and between cultures.

1 Discuss the problems encountered by psychologists in attempts to study lesbian and gay male relations.

2 Consider the differences that exist between individualistic and collectivist cultures, not only in philosophy but in practical terms (such as less mobility in collectivist cultures). How might these have an influence on all types of relationships within the two cultures?

3 List the differences in the characteristics observed in same-sex friendships of men and women. Now consider the different ways in which boys and girls are socialised. Discuss the influence that this differential socialisation may have on same-sex friendship patterns.

Review exercise

Summary

- *Homosexual relationships* have been a neglected area in the field of interpersonal relationships. Some researchers object to the fact that heterosexual relationships have been taken as the standard by which to compare all romantic relationships. We need to be aware that homosexuals are attempting to build relationships in a completely different social context from that of heterosexuals and the difference this makes should not be underestimated.

- *Gender differences in same-sex friendships* emerge at an early age and persist throughout adulthood. Research has indicated that compared to men's friendships, those between women tend to be more intimate, more intense and are generally more important to the people concerned. Women use friendship as a means of sharing confidences; men make friends with people with whom they share activities. No difference has been found in men's ability to be intimate, so the lack of intimacy in their friendships indicates a preference for this style of relating.

  Duck and Wright believe that these differences may have been greatly exaggerated and that both men and women are caring and supportive, and enjoy simply chatting with friends.

- *Cross-cultural differences in heterosexual relationships* can be seen in the approach to marriage. Many researchers distinguish between *individualistic* cultures (most of the Western world), in which *personal goals* are paramount, and *collectivist* cultures (many Eastern countries, including China), in which the emphasis is on *group goals*. In individualistic cultures there is greater individual choice in the marriage partner and the selection is liable to be made on the basis of romantic love. In collectivist cultures there is more likely to be an 'arranged' marriage which involves close relatives having a considerable influence in the selection of marriage partner, a choice which is based largely on occupation and status. Dion and Dion (1993) suggest that the emphasis which individualistic cultures place on independence, personal control and autonomy may make the intimacy expected in Western marriages difficult to achieve and may be a contributor to the high divorce rate.

Further reading

For homosexual relationships

Kitzinger, C. and Coyle, A. (1995) Lesbian and gay couples: speaking of difference, *The Psychologist* 8 (2) (February), 64–9. This article argues that lesbian and gay relationships are often wrongly seen as similar to heterosexual ones and outlines important differences between them.

Wood, J. and Duck, S. (eds) (1995) *Under-studied Relationships*, Thousand Oaks, CA: Sage. Chapter 4, by Huston and Schartz, entitled 'The relationships of lesbians and of gay men', considers the problems of sampling for such research and looks in considerable detail at all aspects of the relationships of homosexuals (including courtship, sex, power and equity, and the impact of the larger society).

For gender differences in same-sex friendships

Miell, D. and Dallos, R. (1996) *Social Interaction and Personal Relationships*, London: Open University Press. See the article by Robert Hinde on 'Gender differences in close relationships' (pp. 324–35).

INDIVIDUAL, SOCIAL, CULTURAL VARIATIONS

For cross-cultural relationships

Goodwin, R. (1995) Personal relationships across cultures, *The Psychologist* 8 (2) (February), 735. This article considers the effects of cultural differences on everyday relationships.

Smith, P.B. and Bond, M.H. (1993) *Social Psychology Across Cultures*, New York: Harvester Wheatsheaf (pp. 138–42). A brief but pertinent look at intimate relationships across cultures.

115

9

Study aids

IMPROVING YOUR ESSAY WRITING SKILLS

At this point in the book you have acquired the knowledge necessary to tackle the exam itself. Answering exam questions is a skill which this chapter shows you how to improve. Examiners have some ideas about what goes wrong in exams. Most importantly, students do not provide this kind of evidence for which the examiner is looking. A grade C answer is typically accurate but has limited detail and commentary, and it is reasonably constructed. To lift such an answer to a grade A or B may require no more than fuller detail, better use of material and a coherent organisation. By studying the essays presented in this chapter, and the examiner's comments, you can learn how to turn grade C answers into grade A. Please note that marks given by the examiner in the practice essays should be used as a guide only and are not definitive. They represent the 'raw marks' given by an AEB examiner. That is, the marks the examiner would give to the examining board based on a total of 24 marks per question broken down into Skill A (description) and Skill B (evaluation). A table showing this scheme is in Appendix C of Paul Humphreys' title in the series, *Exam Success in AEB Psychology*. They may not be the marks given on the examination certificate received ultimately by the student because all examining boards are required to use a common standardised system called the Uniform Mark Scale (UMS) which adjusts all raw scores to a single standard acceptable to all examining boards.

The essays are about the length a student would be able to write in 35–40 minutes (leaving you extra time for planning and checking). Each essay is followed by detailed comments about its strengths and weaknesses. The most common problems to look out for are:

- Failure to answer the actual question set and presenting 'one written during your course'.
- A lack of evaluation, or commentary – many weak essays suffer from this.
- Too much evaluation and not enough description. Description is vital in demonstrating your knowledge and understanding of the selected topic.
- Writing 'everything you know' in the hope that something will get credit. Excellence is displayed through selectivity, and therefore improvements can often be made by *removing* material which is irrelevant to the question set.

For more ideas on how to write good essays you should consult *Exam Success in AEB Psychology* (Paul Humphreys) in this series.

Practice essay 1

Describe and evaluate psychological research into the dissolution (breakdown) of relationships. (24 marks)
[AEB, Summer 1998]

In this essay you will get 12 marks for describing the psychological research into dissolution (breakdown) and 12 marks for evaluating this research.

Candidate's answer

Western relationships are usually voluntary and short-lived and so most people will experience the breakdown of a relationship at some time in their life. This is less likely to happen in non-Western cultures where relationships are obligatory and long-lasting.

Many theories explain the formation of relationships and some of these theories can be used to explain why relationships break down.

Sociobiology states that many of our behaviours can be explained in terms of passing on our genes, just as other animals do. Wilson said that men want to 'spread their seed' to ensure they pass their genes on, whereas women wish to care for the offspring they have and want to tie men down to help them. This theory may help explain the breakdown of a relationship when the male becomes restless and wishes to have many different relationships.

The reinforcement and need satisfaction theory states that we enter relationships in order to have our needs fulfilled and because we gain reinforcement from being in a relationship. This suggests that the breakdown of a relationship is due to the dissatisfaction of one or both partners because their needs are no longer being fulfilled and the relationship is no longer reinforcing.

Social exchange theory and equity theories suggest that we go into relationships to see what we can get out of them. If there is no equality in the relationship and if we are not getting out as much as we are putting in, we become dissatisfied and wish to end the relationship.

There have been many reasons put forward for the breakdown of a relationship such as lack of equality, differing interests, boredom and monotony. If any of these exist in a relationship, people get fed up and wish to end it.

Through research, four stages of the breakdown of a relationship have been identified. In the first stage one partner becomes dissatisfied with the relationship. If this dissatisfaction is made known to the partner, it continues to the next stage where the couple decide to split. During Stage 3 the split is made public and the couple seek friends to give them social support. Stage 4 is the 'grave-dressing' stage where both parties organise their lives without their ex-partner and start to tell their own versions of the relationship.

Research has shown that women have greater social support than men when a relationship breaks down because they have more friends and are closer to their family and rely on people more heavily to recover from the split.

Relationship breakdown has been shown to have a detrimental effect on health and happiness. It has been shown that divorcees are more likely than married people to suffer from mental illness, but this may be the reason why the relationship broke down in the first place.

However, it has also been shown that 75 per cent of divorcees said that they were very happy, compared to a smaller percentage of single people. It has been proved that divorce can make people much happier, as they have been unhappy in their relationship. Many divorced people reported feelings of greater happiness at being single again and many thought they now had more opportunities, since their spouse had been the cause of anxiety.

It has also been shown that women tend to suffer more financially when a relationship ends, as a man is usually the main provider.

Overall, research has told us a lot about relationship breakdown, its causes and its effects on health and happiness. Relationships are a major part of our lives and so relationship breakdown can be very stressful. There is little cross-cultural research on breakdown of relationships, perhaps because non-Western relationships seem to be long-lasting and it is often obligatory to stay in a relationship.

Examiner's comments

As far as description is concerned, this essay has reasonable content: it covers several theories, a model of breakdown and the effects of relationship dissolution on health and happiness. The theories are appropriately used to describe the reasons why relationships may break down. Although not credited to him, Duck's model of the stages of breakdown are briefly and appropriately covered and credit would also be gained for the mention that women have more social support than men after a relationship breaks down. However, there is almost no identification of specified research, no names or dates and very little elaboration, which precludes it coming in the top band. Overall, the descriptive part of the essay would gain about 7 marks out of 12.

The real weakness of this answer is its extremely limited evaluation. After a promising start when there is a little application in the first paragraph (with the reference to cultural differences in breakdown), there then follows almost exclusive description and no evaluation until right near the end. All the theories mentioned – sociobiology, reinforcement and need satisfaction, social exchange, and equity – could be briefly evaluated, and this would have made all the difference to the quality of the answer. For example, sociobiological theory is controversial in its prediction that relationships may break down because men are biologically inclined to 'spread their seed' and therefore to leave their partners. Some would argue that *cultural norms* make it acceptable, indeed may encourage the 'sowing of wild oats'. Remember that the question asked for 'evaluation of research . . .'. There is research to back sociobiological theory but it is not mentioned here, so obviously it is not evaluated. Likewise, research used to support the other theories is not included, so evaluative points like its dubious ecological validity and limited scope are not discussed The candidate would *not* have to describe the studies in detail, but they could evaluate the type of research that has been conducted. There is no mention, either, of the applications or implications of these theories – all good evaluation if included.

The research on the effect of health and happiness of breakdown is commentary, but it's too little too late. This is a great shame, because the candidate has largely ignored the fact that 12 out of the 24 marks are for evaluation and commentary which has clearly been asked for in the question. Therefore, this part of the answer would only gain about 3 marks out of 12.

Overall then, this answer would gain about 10 marks out of 24, around a grade E.

Practice essay 2

(a) **Describe two explanations of the formation of relationships.**

(b) **Assess the extent of cultural variations in the nature of relationships.**

[AEB, January 1998]

In this question, part (a) calls for description only, without evaluation, and gains 12 marks.

Part (b) requires an assessment of the extent to which cultural variations exist in interpersonal relationships and is worth 12 marks. Note that in part (b) you could write about any facet of interpersonal relationships (such as love and intimacy). You do not *have to restrict your answer to cultural variations in the* formation *of relationships but are free to explore any aspects of relationships.*

Candidate's answer

(a) We engage in relationships primarily because we find them rewarding. Argyle said that relationships, especially with spouses, are the greatest source of pleasure in our lives. However, they can also be the greatest source of anguish in our lives.

Argyle, while not part of his own theory, has supported the following concept of the formation of relationships:

- communication: first step to creating a relationship
- contact: meeting with someone, getting to see what they are like
- common interests: on which mutual liking will be based
- compatibility: a definite liking, 'getting on' with someone.

While this is not a theory, Argyle used it as the basis on which to conclude that relationships begin due to three factors:

1 physical attraction
2 familiarity
3 proximity.

These three factors can be applied to any interpersonal relationship, and is arguably a very sound basis on which we form relationships in our everyday lives. Other factors have also been added to these three considerations of formation:

- perceived similarity
- reciprocal liking
- complementarity
- competence.

These are just as valid as Argyle's first three factors. However, a relationship may be formed in our Western society of 'if I can't see it, I don't know I'll like it' by using Argyle's first three factors only, unlike non-Western cultures where none of the factors above are applicable to the formation of relationships.

Levinger also produced a model to describe the five phases we pass through in a relationship. This model is:

1 Acquaintance
2 Buildup
3 Consolidation

4 Deterioration
5 Ending.

This is more commonly known as his ABCDE model. From this model, the first two phases are a valid theory as to the formation of relationships. Acquaintance has to occur before any type of relationship can be formed and determines the fate of the encounter – does it continue, or does it stop immediately? If the decision to continue has been made, the formation of the relationship moves into the 'Buildup' phase, where ties and immediate likes and dislikes are formed, and where initial negotiation between the parties for rewards, etc. takes place (as in Walster *et al.*'s equity theory where the first act to take place in a relationship is the negotiation for rewards, i.e. love, sex, respect, status: Foa and Foa).

(b) Cultural variations in relationships are very marked between Western and non-Western cultures. Moghaddam *et al.* have done much to highlight the very wide differences between the way people form relationships in the West and how relationships are formed in the East.

In the West, relationships are very much based upon individual choice and preference, with little (if any) interference from other parties such as parents. Geography may also play a deciding factor in the viability of a relationship, but this may be seen as inconsequential compared to the polar opposite methods used in non-Western culture. Non-Western cultures are family/kin-orientated, with the whole family deciding and influencing all the social and interpersonal relationships of the younger or single members of the family.

Moghaddam *et al.* put forward the following theory. Western cultures form relationships that are:

- individualistic (chosen by the individual)
- voluntary (choice is an option)
- temporary (can be terminated at any time).

However, non-Western cultures approach relationships in an entirely different way. Their relationships are:

- multiple (chosen by many for one person)
- obligatory (no choice as to who you marry)
- permanent (no possibility of termination).

While to the Western culture this may seem unfair, some psychologists see it as a good reason to encourage working through the bad patches of relationships instead of ending them.

In addition, the Western approach to relationships assumes there has to be option to terminate and this may have an effect on mental health, for example, divorce (Cochrane pointed out that divorced people are seven times more likely to be mentally ill). However, mental health problems are substantially lower in non-Western than Western cultures and this can be put down to the very strong kin/family/social support network that their culture provides.

Argyle also points out that Western relationships put a pressure on people that unhappiness must automatically follow the termination of a relationship and, where death occurs, this may be true. But some people are genuinely happy to have finished a relationship.

So whereas the non-Western culture does not have a get-out clause, it does have a strong support structure for bad times. In Western cultures we don't have the support of a large family network that has been involved in our relationships from inception, but we do have the option to terminate the relationship, which may be a good option, especially where the relationship is violent.

Examiner's comments

Part (a): when, as in this example, you are asked for a *specific number* of explanations, then it is always wise to make it crystal clear where one stops and another starts. It is also wise to outline in the introduction exactly which explanations (or theories, etc.) you intend to use. In this answer, it is not very clear exactly which two particular explanations are being discussed. Much of the early part of the answer is an appropriate explanation but this is not very well expressed, partly because it is written in note form which is never a good idea. Certain important and relevant factors are listed (physical attractiveness, familiarity, proximity) but no *explanation* is provided of how these factors affect the formation of a relationship. Remember: the question specifically asks for explanations, not just descriptions of the formation of friendships.

The brief coverage of Levinger does gain a little credit for mentioning the fact that during buildup, rewards take place.

Since the explanations are covered rather superficially, mainly in the form of lists of factors, this part of the answer, would gain about 6 marks out of a possible 12.

In order to gain a good mark, it is necessary to first make a clear decision as to which two explanations you intend to cover and describe each one clearly. The theories covered in Chapter 3 would provide suitable explanations: reinforcement affect theory, social exchange theory, equity theory and sociobiology. Remember to be clear exactly which two explanations you are describing and do not introduce any others, because you will only get credit for two.

Part (b): The answer to this part of the question is much better than the first part. It states which cultural variations will be discussed (that between East and West) and clearly lays out the major characteristics of the relationships in both East and West. It then goes on to point out the advantages and disadvantages of each of these approaches as the basis for relationships, including the option to terminate, and both positive and negative effects of divorce. It does tend to be a little repetitive but it is reasonably well informed and coherent. This part of the answer would gain about 8 marks out of 12.

So how could it be improved? It would be a better answer if the student did not polarise the differences between East and West (he or she has actually talked about one approach being the 'polar opposite' of the other). One is given the impression that in Western societies people have a totally free choice (only limited if you are a minor) and in Eastern cultures people have no choice at all. Even a superficial look at relationships reveals that people in the West are greatly influenced in their choice of marriage partner by parental and cultural expectations, even if this is implicit; similarly, few people in the East have no choice whatsoever in their marriage partner. As mentioned in Chapter 8, we must not confuse arranged marriages with forced marriages, the latter being relatively rare. Another improvement would be an elaboration of the characteristics of cultures which lead to these differences in approach to relationships. There is a tendency in many student essays to present information in the form of a list. Although this is a good way to write out your notes in order to learn them, it does not give a good structure to an essay, nor does it lend itself to appropriate elaboration. As you can see, this candidate has resorted to comments in brackets after each characteristic. If you do this, you will gain good marks for information (content) but not for good and appropriate structuring.

In total then, this answer gains 14 out of 24 marks, a borderline B/C grade.

Practice essay 3

Discuss some of the effects that interpersonal relationships have been shown to have on a person's psychological well-being (e.g. happiness and health). (24 marks)

[AEB Summer 1997]

Candidate's answer

Having relationships, whether they are of an intimate kind or not, is very important. To know that you are able to turn to someone is very comforting.

Happiness is related to the married rather than to the single. Married people are happier than those who are divorced or single and they live longer. This means, presumably, that they are healthier as well. Having said that, some people are quite relieved to escape a relationship but they are unlikely to be happy, just less miserable than they were before.

Divorce tends to make men more unhappy than it makes women. Women tend to turn to friends for social support when they are breaking up a relationship (it's usually the woman who breaks it up, especially if the relationship is marriage). Men look for another person to marry – remarriage in men is much quicker than in women but it often does not work. Divorce in second marriages is higher than in first ones.

The reason why men get remarried again is suggested by psychologists to be because they don't have such good friendships as women and they cannot pour out their hearts because they don't like talking about intimate matters. This shows that people do need relationships and do not like being on their own. Women seem to have support from friends, men from marriage, so it's different for the two sexes. But they each need relationships – just different types.

Stress to a person has been shown to have a major effect on health. The happiest people are those who don't worry about things and this is related to the married rather than the single. If a person suffers from stress or strain from a relationship, it could lead to illness such as flu, common colds or fevers. It is known that stress has an enormous effect on the immune system. On the other hand, the help and support that is offered by a relationship may make the stress a lot less. Married people have been found to recover from serious illness much better than single people. This may be because the spouse looks after you or because just knowing they are there for you and care about you makes you feel better and less stressed and get better quicker.

Losing a loved one or even a very close friend could prove to be an enormous strain to cope with. This would probably ensure a decrease in the level of general health because there would be a lack of concern for things such as eating, neglecting things done for survival such as drinking, eating, keeping up with hygiene levels. This could affect the health of a person greatly.

Divorced and separated people are more likely to be mentally ill or commit suicide than married people.

Examiner's comments

Although this essay does contain a little relevant information, it is badly structured and rambling. You get the impression that the candidate is not at all confident in this particular area and is making it up as they go along. However little (or however much) you know about a topic area, it is worth spending time *doing a plan* so that the information can be appropriately organised. In this essay, the candidate goes back and forward between health and happiness without any sense of direction. The effects of divorce and separation are spattered around and there is no sense of a real introduction or conclusion. The description part of this essay would gain about 6 marks out of 12 because, although it is generally accurate, it is quite limited in content and lacking in detail.

There is a notable lack of evaluation and commentary in this essay. Although there is brief mention of how relationships affect health and happiness, it is very rudimentary. Likewise the comments on the sex differences, although these are a little more developed.

What is notable by its absence is any consideration of why there is a relationship between health and happiness on the one hand and marriage on the other. We need at least to consider (even if we eventually reject) the notion that it is not being married that *causes* people to be healthier and happier, but that it is healthy and happy people who choose to marry or are chosen as partners. Likewise, people may get divorced *because* they are depressed, mentally ill or drinking a great deal of alcohol rather than depressed, mentally ill or drinking a lot of alcohol *because of* the divorce. There is some evidence that this may not be the case but neither the argument nor the evidence in either direction is presented by the candidate. With regard to health, the notion of it having a 'buffering' effect is never entertained by this candidate. As well as information, you need commentary in order to obtain good marks.

There are many interpersonal relationships in life but this candidate concentrates largely (but, to be fair, not exclusively) on marriage. This is understandable, given the nature of the research, but in a good essay that should be acknowledged.

Since the evaluation/commentary part of this essay is superficial and the evaluation of the link between relationships and psychological well-being is basic and lacks depth, it would only gain about 4 marks out of 12 for this skill domain. The total essay mark, then, is 10 out of 24, about a grade E.

KEY RESEARCH SUMMARY

Article 1

'Importance of physical attractiveness in dating behaviour', Elaine Walster, Vera Aronson, Darcy Abrahams and Leon Rottmann in *Journal of Personality and Social Psychology* (1966) 4 (5), 508–16.

Introduction

This study was a field experiment in which couples were matched in a giant 'computer date' arrangement. There were three hypotheses tested:

1 That individuals who are socially desirable (in terms of physical attraction, being personable or having a wealth of material possessions) will require greater social desirability in a partner than people who are less socially desirable.

2 If couples who vary in social desirability meet in a social situation, those couples who are similar in social desirability will most often attempt to date one another.

3 Individuals will not only choose to date people of equal desirability, they will like those people most.

Method

Before the dance

An advertisement was posted inviting new students to buy tickets for a special dance in which they would be paired by computer with a member of the opposite sex. The dance was part of 'Welcome Week' entertainments – events provided for incoming students at the University of Minnesota.

When the students went to buy their tickets, four confederates secretly rated them on physical attractiveness (which was the only measure of social desirability that was made). The assessment was deliberately done very quickly, within one or two seconds, in order that no other qualities, such as personableness or intelligence, were taken into consideration. An 8-point rating scale was used, from 1 (extremely unattractive) to 8 (extremely attractive).

After buying their tickets, the students completed a questionnaire that was supposedly to be used for matching purposes. Dates were, in fact, assigned randomly with one proviso: that the man should be taller than the woman. They were then sent the name of their date and were advised to meet for the first time at the dance, but many couples arranged to meet at the girl's home and arrived at the dance together.

During the dance

Of the 376 couples who had purchased tickets, 332 couples attended. During the intermission, men and women were asked to go to separate rooms where they were requested to complete a questionnaire assessing their dates and the dance itself. The information was strictly confidential but the ticket numbers were noted (each member of a pair had the same number). Participants were encouraged to answer all questions honestly. All but five of the 332 couples attending the dance completed the questionnaire, either during the intermission or when contacted two days later. Hence data were based on 327 couples.

The main factors on which participants were asked to comment were:

(a) How much they liked their date.
(b) How physically attractive and personally attractive was the date.
(c) How similar were the date's attitudes, values and beliefs to their own.
(d) Whether the individual would like to meet their date again.

After the date

A follow-up was conducted four to six months later to ascertain whether participants had tried to date their computer date after the dance. Ten couples could not be contacted.

The final sample was therefore 317 couples.

RESULTS

Hypothesis 1: The more attractive the individuals were, the less attractive they rated their date and the less likely they were to want to see their date again. Hence, hypothesis 1, that individuals who are socially desirable (in terms of physical attraction, being personable or having a wealth of material possessions) will require greater social desirability in a partner than people who are less socially desirable, was confirmed with regard to both men and women.

Hypotheses 2 and 3: These were tested together. They both corresponded to the 'matching hypothesis', stating (a) that individuals would most often choose to date a partner of similar attractiveness to themselves, and (b) that given a choice of various levels of attractiveness, people would prefer someone of a similar level of attractiveness.

Neither of these hypotheses was supported. Men did not attempt only to date people of similar attractiveness. The only important determinant of whether or not the date was asked out again was how attractive the date was: the most attractive girls were the most often asked out. This was generally true regardless of the attractiveness of the man who asked her out. There was **not** a significant tendency for participants to date partners of approximately their own physical desirability.

Hypothesis 3 was also unsupported. Rather than liking an individual who was equal in attractiveness, one rule prevailed: regardless of sex, the more attractive the individual, the better they were liked. The researchers had assumed that physical attractiveness would be a much less important determinant for women in their rating of men than vice versa – but they were wrong.

LIMITATIONS The findings were limited in several ways. The setting used was a large group situation in which contact between individuals was brief. Perhaps as they got to know each other over a longer period of time, similarity of attitudes, interests and beliefs would become more important than physical attractiveness. The results were also based on a sample of 18-year-olds and therefore not generalisable to an older population for whom shared values may be more important.

CONCLUSION The only important determinant of a person's liking for their date was that person's physical attractiveness.

Article 2

'Men as success objects and women as sex objects: a study of personal advertisements', Simon Davis in *Sex Roles* (1990) 23 (1/2), 43–50.

Introduction

Previous research indicates that in their choice of long-term sexual partner, men tend to emphasise physical attractiveness and sexuality to a greater extent than do women, and this has been shown in more than one culture (Stiles *et al.*, 1987). Women, in contrast, tend to emphasise psychological and personality characteristics and seek a long-term, committed relationship. They also place greater emphasis than men on seeking financial security from a partner.

Previous research indicated that these different priorities were reflected in 'lonely hearts' advertisements. Harrison *et al.* (1977) found that women were more likely to seek financial security and men were more likely to seek attractiveness. Similar results were found by Deaux and Lewis (1984), who also found that women were more likely than men to stress the importance of longevity and quality in a relationship.

This study looked at the characteristics emphasised in personal advertisements in newspapers, this time in Canadian ones. It examined in particular whether traditional stereotypes were in operation; that is, women being viewed as sex objects and men as success objects (success being measured in terms of intellectual achievements and financial accomplishments).

Method

Personal advertisements were taken from six Saturday editions of the *Vancouver Sun* (taken throughout each season over a year). All advertisements seeking heterosexual partners were included, but only those parts of the advertisement referring to the characteristics sought in a partner were included in the analysis (for example, hobbies and interests of the advertiser were excluded).

The attributions listed in the advertisements were coded as follows:

1 *Attractive*: specified that a person should be, for example, 'pretty' or 'handsome'.
2 *Physique*: specified that the partner should, for example, be 'fit and trim', 'muscular' or 'have a good figure'.
3 *Sex*: specified that the partner should have, for instance, 'high sex drive' or be 'sensuous' or 'erotic'.
4 *Picture*: specified that the person should send a picture or photograph.
5 *Professional*: specified that the partner should be a professional.
6 *Employed*: for example, 'must hold steady job'.
7 *Financial*: specified that the partner should be, for example, financially secure or financially independent.

8 *Education*: specified that the partner should be, for example, 'a college grad.' 'well educated'.
9 *Intelligence*: specified that the partner should be 'intelligent', 'bright'.
10 *Honest*: specified that the partner should be 'honest' or 'have integrity'.
11 *Humour*: specified 'sense of humour', 'cheerfulness'.
12 *Commitment*: specified that the relationship was to be 'long term' or 'lead to marriage'.
13 *Emotion*: specified that the partner should be 'warm', 'romantic', 'emotionally supportive', 'sensitive', 'loving', 'responsive'.

In addition to these thirteen attributes, two other pieces of information were collected: the length of the advertisement and the age of the person placing it (if age was vague, it was not included).

Scoring

If any of the thirteen attributes mentioned above was mentioned it was scored once, regardless of how many times it was mentioned in the single advertisement.

A chi-squared analysis was carried out, with male/female on one dimension and attribute (asked for/not asked for) on the other. (This meant thirteen chi-squared tests were carried out during this part of the analysis, each 2 x 2, male/female x attribute asked for/not asked for).

Several of the individual variables were then combined in order to get an impression of the overall importance of (a) physical factors (attributes 1–4), (b) employment factors (attributes 5–7), (c) intellectual factors (attributes 8 and 9).

RESULTS

A total of 328 advertisements were used (no gay advertisements were included): 215 (65.5 per cent) placed by men, 113 (34.5 per cent) by women. Mean age of advertisers was 40.4 years, similar for men and women. The table on p. 134 summarised the results.

As this table shows, ten of the thirteen attributes were significant. The three largest differences were for attractiveness and professional and financial status. With regard to attractiveness, physique, sex, and

	Gender				
Variable	Desired by men		Desired by women		P	(chi-squared)
Attractive	76	(35.5%)	20	(17.7%)	<0.05	(11.13)
Physique	81	(37.7%)	27	(23.9%)	<0.05	(6.37)
Sex	25	(11.6%)	4	(3.5%)	<0.05	(6.03)
Picture	74	(34.4%)	24	(21.2%)	<0.05	(6.18)
Professional	6	(2.8%)	19	(16.8%)	<0.05	(20.74)
Employed	8	(3.7%)	12	(10.6%)	<0.05	(6.12)
Financial	7	(3.2%)	22	(19.5%)	<0.05	(24.26)
Education	8	(3.7%)	8	(7.1%)	NS	(1.79)
Intelligence	22	(10.2%)	24	(21.2%)	<0.05	(7.46)
Honest	20	(9.3%)	17	(15.0%)	NS	(2.44)
Humour	36	(16.7%)	26	(23.0%)	NS	(1.89)
Commitment	38	(17.6%)	31	(27.4%)	<0.05	(4.25)
Emotion	44	(20.5%)	35	(31.0%)	<0.05	(4.36)

NS= not significant

whether or not a picture was requested, the men were more likely than the women to seek these. In the case of professional status, employment status, financial status, intelligence commitment and emotion, the women were more likely to seek these. The women were also more likely to specify education, honesty and humour, but not a statistically significant level.

With regard to the collapsed categories:

1 Physical categories (attributes 1–4) were significantly more often requested by men
2 Employment categories (attributes 5–7) were significantly more often requested by women

3 Intellectual categories (attributes 8 and 9) were significantly more
   often desired by women.

One final and important finding is *that physical characteristics were
the most desired attributes for both men and women.*

DISCUSSION The results showed that both sexes adhered to
stereotypical sex role requirements. Men were more likely to
emphasise appearance as a desired characteristic in female partners,
but not financial and intellectual status, while women sought men of
high intellect, secure financial status and those who were prepared to
commit.

There are methodological limitations with a content analysis of
this type. People placing personal advertisements cannot be assumed
to be representative of the public in general. The mean age of the
group was 40, which is not typical of the courting situation, and
we therefore have to consider that age is a confounding variable.
Older single people do not necessarily have the same requirements in
a partner as do younger people and we therefore cannot necessarily
generalise too broadly from these results.

QUESTIONS TO CONSIDER

1 How do the results of this study correspond to the sociobiological
   theory of mate selection? (Discussed in Chapter 3.)
2 In what ways may age be a confounding variable in such a study?
   How might the preferences of an older person differ from those of
   a younger person when seeking a heterosexual partner?
3 In the above study, nearly twice as many men as women placed
   advertisements. Can you suggest any reason for this difference?

Article 3

**'An exploratory study of love and liking and type of
marriages', Usha Gupta and Pushpa Singh (University of
Rajasthan, Jaipur), *Indian Journal of Applied Psychology*
(1982) 19 (2), 92–7.**

Introduction

As a result of Westernisation and industrialisation, many changes have occurred in traditional Indian patterns of life. In particular, the education of women has brought about a metamorphosis in the concept of marriage.

In Indian society, love marriages are not uncommon but arranged marriages are still prevalent and preferred in society. The common belief is that love marriages are more successful in the early stages whereas arranged marriages are more successful in the long term with regard to love and liking. This common belief, however, has no empirical foundation.

The study reported here aimed to investigate the effect of type of marriage, duration of marriage and sex (male or female) on love and liking.

Method

The sample used comprised fifty married couples, twenty-five of whose marriages had been arranged and twenty-five who had contracted love marriages. Each of the two groups of twenty-five couples comprised:

- five who had been married for one year or under
- five who had been married for between one and two years
- five who had been married for between two and five years
- five who had been married for between five and ten years
- five who had been married for ten years or more.

The subjects lived just outside Jaipur city and were all graduates with nuclear families.

Rubin's scales of love and liking were administered to all 100 subjects. There were nine items on the love scale and eight on the liking scale. Both scales were rated on a Likert 9-point scale.

RESULTS Opposite are two of the four tables taken from the original paper.

Mean scores for love				
Duration	Male		Female	
in years	Love	Arranged	Love	Arranged
0–1	71.6	53	68.8	62.8
1–2	74.2	60.6	73	65.4
2–5	73.6	70	73.4	68
5–10	56	70.2	51.2	69.6
10 and above	42	70.8	38.2	65.4

Mean scores for liking				
Duration	Male		Female	
in years	Love	Arranged	Love	Arranged
0–1	65.5	55.4	65.0	57.6
1–2	64.8	56.0	65.8	58.4
2–5	62.8	64.2	62.6	65.6
5–10	56.8	65.6	63.6	68.6
10 and above	54.2	61.4	66.8	64.0

As the two tables show, love tends to start at a high level and show a marked decrease in love marriages, whereas in arranged marriages the opposite applies: love starts at a relatively low level and increases (more for males than for females). As far as liking is concerned, the same pattern emerges, but the difference between the new and established marriages is not as extreme as it is on the love scales.

A shortened version of the statistical analysis of results is as follows:

Analysis of variance of love	
	P
Between sex	NS
Between type of marriage	<.05
Between duration	<.01
Sex × type of marriage	NS
Sex × duration	NS
Type of marriage × duration	<.05
Sex × type of marriage × duration	NS

Analysis of variance of liking	
	P
Between sex	<.01
Between type of marriage	NS
Between duration	NS
Sex × type of marriage	NS
Sex × duration	NS
Type of marriage × duration	<.01
Sex × type of marriage × duration	<.05

NS= not significant

Statistical analysis showed that the type of marriage has a significant impact on love but not on liking. Overall, more love is shown in arranged marriages than in love marriages.

Similarly, duration has a significant effect on love but not on liking. As time passes, love and liking decrease between love marriage pairs but it increases between arranged marriage pairs. This difference is significant for love but not for liking.

Overall, females seem to like their husbands more than their husbands like them. In contrast, husbands tend to love their wives more than their wives love them (although the difference is quite small and not significant). The authors comment that Rubin (1970) also found that men tend to be more likeable than women but not more lovable.

CONCLUSION Type of marriage, duration and sex play an important role in love and liking. Harlow (1958) wrote that as far as describing love is concerned, psychologists have failed in their mission. We now need to address this failure. Rubin's scale of love and liking is a first attempt and the paper reported here has built on this in a further bid to throw light on the concept of love and liking.

Glossary

The first occurrence of each of these terms is highlighted in **bold** type in the main text.

affiliation The desire or motivation to seek out the company of other people, regardless of your feelings towards them.

attachment An enduring emotional bond between two people; often used to refer to the emotional relationship between an infant and a particular caregiver.

attachment style The way in which a person typically interacts with those who are significant in their lives. This reflects the mother–infant relationship and may have been secure, avoidant or ambivalent.

attributions The hypotheses we make as to the causes of others' behaviour. These are usually classified as external (due to circumstances) or internal (due to personality).

buffer effect of social support The effect that those people who feel they have social support from others are less affected by stressful events than those who feel unsupported.

classical conditioning A process whereby a previously neutral stimulus becomes associated with a stimulus that evokes a particular response, and thereafter elicits that same response. It therefore involves learning by association.

collectivist society A society that emphasises interdependence, cooperation and social harmony and in which these take priority over individual and personal goals.

companionate love The affection we feel for those with whom our lives are deeply entwined.

comparison level In Thibaut and Kelley's version of social exchange theory, this is the standard used by individuals to judge whether the outcomes of a relationship are satisfactory or unsatisfactory. This standard depends on social norms and personal expectations.

comparison level for alternatives In Thibaut and Kelley's version of social exchange theory, this is the minimum level of outcomes that someone will accept from a relationship taking account of the alternatives available.

correlation A method of establishing whether there is a relationship between two variables. A correlation is positive when both variables increase or decrease together; it is negative when, as one variable increases, the other decreases.

dependent variable A behaviour that is measured in an experiment to see whether it has been affected by the independent variable.

ecological validity The extent to which a finding or theory applies to everyday life.

equity theory A theory which proposes that the amount of satisfaction people expect from a relationship is in proportion to their initial investment and that, if this is not so, they will be dissatisfied and act to try and restore equity.

exchange orientation An attitude in which people expect an equal exchange of equity within a relationship.

expressive friendship A friendship based on emotional sharing, typical of female–female relationships.

field studies Studies that take place in everyday settings that have not been designed for research.

filter theory When referring to interpersonal relationships, a filter theory proposes that when we choose a partner, we pass through a series of stages in which we successively narrow down our choices.

functional distance The likelihood of two people coming into contact.

independent variable The factor manipulated in an experiment to see if it affects the dependent variable.

individualistic society A society in which there is great emphasis on the rights, values and interests of the individual and in which these beliefs determine the social norms and values of that society.

instrumental friendship A friendship based on sharing of common activities, typical of male–male friendships.

law of attraction There is a direct linear relationship between the level of attraction and the proportion of similar attitudes (that is, the number of similar attitudes divided by the total number of similar and dissimilar attitudes).

matching hypothesis People tend to choose as friends and lovers those people who are equivalent to them, particularly in terms of physical attractiveness but also in terms of such characteristics as intelligence, background and attitudes.

operant conditioning Learning that takes place when a response is followed by a reinforcer, resulting in an increase in the frequency of the response. It involves learning by consequences.

opportunity sample A sample chosen because they are easily available.

passionate love A powerful emotional state that involves overwhelming feelings of tenderness, anxiety and sexual desire.

principle of least interest This states that in a relationship it is the person who is less interested who has the greater influence and power.

proportional hypothesis The higher the proportion of similar attitudes, the greater the liking. The proportion is determined by the number of similar attitudes divided by the total number of attitudes on which views are expressed.

reinforcement–affect theory A theory of interpersonal attraction which proposes that we like people who reward us and with whom we associate pleasant experiences.

repulsion hypothesis Dissimilar attitudes decrease attraction but similar attitudes have no effect.

self-disclosure Revelations about personal information that one person makes to another.

self-fulfilling prophecy The process by which expectations about a person eventually become true due to the fact that he or she is treated in a way that influences them to behave according to these expectations.

social comparison theory Festinger's theory that people prefer to compare themselves with others in order to assess the appropriateness of their own thoughts, beliefs or feelings.

social exchange theory People seek to maximise rewards and minimise costs in their relationships with others.

social penetration theory As a relationship deepens, self-disclosures become broader (include more topic areas) and deeper (more intimate).

sociobiology A (controversial) approach that argues that much of human social behaviour is biologically determined.

stimulus–value–role model Murstein's model that suggests that selecting a sexual partner occurs in three stages: the stimulus stage, the value stage and the role stage.

Bibliography

Adams, R.G. (1986) Friendship and aging, *Generations* 10, 40–3.

Ainsworth, M., Blehar, M.C., Waters, E. and Wall, S. (1978) *Patterns of Attachment: A Psychological Study of the Strange Situation*, Hillsdale, NJ: Erlsbaum.

Altman, I., Vinsel, A. and Brown, B.A. (1981) Dialectic conceptions in social psychology: an application to social penetration and privacy regulation, in L. Berkowitz (ed.), *Advances in Experimental Social Psychology* (vol. 14), New York: Academic Press.

Altman, L. and Taylor, D.A. (1973) *Social Penetration*, New York: Holt, Rinehart, Winston.

Argyle, M. (1988) *Bodily Communication*, New York: Methuen.

Argyle, M. and Henderson, M. (1985) *The Anatomy of Relationships*, Harmondsworth: Penguin.

Argyle, M., Henderson, M. and Furnham, A. (1985) The rules of social relationships, *British Journal of Social Psychology* 24, 125–39.

Aronson, E. and Linder, D. (1965) Gain and loss of esteem as determinants of interpersonal attractiveness, *Journal of Experimental Social Psychology* 1, 156–72.

Aronson, E. and Worchel, S. (1966) Similarity versus liking as determinants of interpersonal attractiveness, *Psychonomic Science* 5, 157–8.

Backman, C.W. and Secord, P.F. (1959) The effect of perceived liking on interpersonal attraction, *Human Relations* 12, 379–84.

Bank, S. (1992) Remembering and reinterpreting sibling bonds, in F. Boer and J. Dunn (eds), *Children's Sibling Relationships: Developmental and Clinical Issues*, Hillsdale, NJ: Erlbaum.

Baron, R.A. and Thomley, J. (1992) Positive affect as a potential mediator of the effects of pleasant fragrances on work-related behaviour, *Journal of Applied Social Psychology* 23, 1179–203.

Baudonniere, P-M. (1987) Interactions dyadiques entre enfants de 4 ans: inconnus, familiers et amis. Le rôle du degrée de familiarité, *International Journal of Psychology* 22, 347–62.

Baxter, L.A. (1984) Trajectories of relationship dissengagement, *Journal of Social and Personal Relationships* 1, 29–48.

Beach, S.R.H. and Tesser, A. (1993) Decision making power and marital satisfaction: a self-evaluation maintenance perspective, *Journal of Social and Clinical Psychology* 12, 471–94.

Becker, C.S. (1988) *Unbroken Ties: Lesbian Ex-lovers*, Boston, MA: Alyson.

Bee, H. (1992) *The Developing Child* (6th edn), New York: HarperCollins.

Berkman, L. and Syme, S. (1979) Social networks, host resistance, and mortality: a nine year followup study of Alameda County residents, *American Journal of Epidemiology* 109, 186–204.

Berman, J.J., Murphy-Berman, V. and Singh, P. (1985) Cross-cultural similarities and differences in perceptions of fairness, *Journal of Cross-Cultural Psychology* 16, 55–67.

Berscheid, E. (1983) Emotion, in H.H. Kelley, E. Berscheid, A. Christensen, J.H. Harvey, T.L. Huston, G. Levinger, E. McClintock, L.A. Peplau and D.R. Peterson (eds), *Close Relationships*, New York: Freeman, 110–68.

Berscheid, E. and Walster, E. (1969) *Interpersonal Attraction*, Reading, MA: Addison-Wesley.

Berscheid, E. and Walster, E. (1978) *Interpersonal Attraction* (2nd edn), Reading, MA: Addison-Wesley.

Berscheid, E., Synder, M. and Omoto, A.M. (1989) The relationship closeness inventory: assessing the closeness of interpersonal relationships, *Journal of Personality and Social Psychology* 57, 792–807.

Bloom, B., Asher, S.J. and White, S.W. (1978) Marital disruption as a stressor: a review and analysis, *Psychological Bulletin* 85, 867–94.

Blumstein, P. and Schwartz, P. (1983) *American Couples: Money, Work, Sex*, New York: Morrow.

Bossard, J.H.S. (1932) Residential propinquity as a factor in marriage selection, *American Journal of Sociology* 38, 219–24.

Bradbury, T.N. and Fincham, F.D. (1990) Attributions in marriage: review and critique, *Psychological Bulletin* 107, 3–33.

Braiker, H.B. and Kelley, H.H. (1979) Conflict in the development of close relationships, in R.L. Burgess and T.L. Huston (eds), *Social Exchange in Developing Relationships*, New York and London: Academic Press.

Brehm, S.S. (1992) *Intimate Relationships*, New York: McGraw-Hill, Inc.

Brown, G.W. and Harris, T. (1978) *Social Origins of Depression*, London: Tavistock.

Buhrmester, D. and Furman, W. (1987) The development of companionship and intimacy, *Child Development* 58, 1101–13.

Burnstein, E., Crandall, C. and Kitayama, S. (1994) Some neo-Darwinian roles for altruism: weighing cues for inclusive fitness as function of the biological importance of the decision, *Journal of Personality and Social Psychology* 67, 773–89.

Burr, W.R. (1970) Satisfaction with various aspects of marriage over the life cycle: a random middle class sample, *Journal of Marriage and the Family* 32, 29–37.

Buss, D.M. (1985) Human mate selection, *American Scientist* 73, 47–51.

—— (1989) Sex differences in human mate preferences: evolutionary hypotheses tested in 37 cultures, *Behavioral and Brain Sciences* 12, 1–14.

Buunk, B.P. (1987) Conditions that promote break-ups as a consequence of extradyadic involveness, *Journal of Social and Clinical Psychology* 5, 237–50.

—— (1996) Affiliation, attraction and close relationships, in M. Hewstone, W. Stroebe and G.M. Stephenson (eds), *Introduction to Social Psychology* (2nd edn), Oxford: Blackwell.

Buunk, B.P. and VanYperen, N.W. (1991) Referential comparison, relational comparisons and exchange orientation: their relation to marital satisfaction, *Personality and Social Psychology Bulletin* 17, 710–18.

Byrne, D. (1971) *The Attraction Paradigm*, New York: Academic Press.

Byrne, D. and Clore, G.L. (1970) A reinforcement model of evaluative processes, *Personality: An International Journal* 1, 103–28.

Byrne, D., Clore, G.L. and Smeaton, G. (1986) The attraction hypothesis: do similar attitudes affect anything?, *Journal of Personality and Social Psychology* 51, 1167–70.

Campbell, A., Converse, P.E. and Rodgers, W.L. (1976) *The Quality of American Life*, New York: Russell Sage Foundation.

Campell, A. (1981) The sense of well-being in America: patterns and trends, New York: McGraw-Hill.

Cate, R.M. and Lloyd, S.A. (1988) Courtship, in S. Duck (ed.), *Handbook of Personal Relationships: Theory, Research and Intervention*, New York: Wiley, 409–27.

Cate, R.M. and Lloyd, S.A. (1992) *Courtship*, Newbury Park, CA: Sage.

Cate, R.M., Lloyd, S.A. and Long, E. (1988) The role of rewards and fairness in developing premarital relationships, *Journal of Marriage and the Family* 50, 443–52.

Cattell, R.B. and Nesselrode, J.R. (1967). Likeness and completeness theories examined by 16 personality factor measures on stable and unstable married couples, *Journal of Personality and Social Psychology* 7, 351–61.

Chapman, B. (1992) The Byrne–Clore formula revisited: the additional impact of number of dissimilar attitudes on attraction, unpublished Masters thesis, University at Albany, State University of New York.

Clark, M.S. and Mills, J. (1979) Interpersonal attraction in exchange and communal relationships, *Journal of Personality and Social Psychology* 37, 12–24.

Clore, G.L. and Byrne, D. (1974) A reinforcement model of attraction, in T.I. Huston (ed.), *Foundations of Interpersonal Attraction*, New York: Academic Press, 143–70.

Cohen, S. and Hoberman, H.M. (1982) Positive events and social supports as buffers on life change stress: maximising the prediction of health outcome, unpublished, University of Oregon.

Cole, C.L. (1984) Marital quality in later life, in W.H. Quinn and G.H. Highston (eds), *Independent Aging: Family and Social Support Perspectives*, Gaithersburg, MD: Aspen, 72–90.

Cook, E. (1997) Is marriage driving women mad?, *Independent on Sunday*, 10 August.

Cooper, G. (1996) The satisfying side of being home alone, *Independent*, 13 September.

Cramer, D. (1987) Lovestyles revisited, *Social Behaviour and Personality* 15, 215–18.

—— (1995) Personal relationships, *The Psychologist* 8 (2) (February).

—— (1998) *Close Relationships: The Study of Love and Friendship*, Arnold.

Cunningham, M.R. (1986) Measuring the physical in physical attractiveness: quasi-experiments on the sociobiology of female facial beauty, *Journal of Personality and Social Psychology* 50 (5), 925–35.

Curtis, R.C. and Miller, K. (1986) Believing another likes or dislikes you: behaviors making the beliefs come true, *Journal of Personality and Social Psychology* 51, 284–90.

Davis, S. (1990) Men as success objects and women as sex objects: a study of personal advertisements, *Sex Roles* 23, 43–50.

Deaux, K. and Lewis, L. (1984) The structure of gender stereotypes: interrelationships among components and gender label, *Journal of Personality and Social Psychology* 52, 991–1004.

Derlega, V.J., Metts, S., Petronio, S. and Margulis, S.T. (1993) *Self-disclosure*, Newbury Park, CA: Sage.

Dermer, M. and Thiel, D.L. (1975) When beauty may fail, *Journal of Personality and Social Psychology* 31, 1168–76.

Deutsch, M. and Collins, M.E. (1951) *Interracial Housing: A Psychological Evaluation of a Social Experiment*, Minneapolis: University of Minnesota Press.

De Waal, F. (1983) *Chimpanzee Politics: Power and Sex Among Apes*, New York: Harper & Row.

Dindia, K. and Allen, M. (1992) Sex differences in self disclosure: a meta-analysis, *Psychological Bulletin* 112, 106–24.

Dion, K.K. and Berscheid, E. (1974) Physical attractiveness and peer perception among children, *Sociometry* 37, 1–12.

Dion, K.K. and Dion, K.L. (1993) Individualistic and collectivist perspectives on gender and the cultural context of love and intimacy, *Journal of Social Issues* 49(3), 53–69.

Duck, S.W. (1982) *Personal Relationships 4: Dissolving Personal Relationships*, London and New York: Academic Press.

—— (1984) A perspective on the repair of personal relationships: repair of what, when?, in S.W. Duck (ed.), *Personal Relationships 5: Repairing Personal Relationships*, London: Academic Press.

—— (1988) *Relating to Others*, Milton Keynes: Open University Press.

—— (1992) *Human Relationships* (2nd edn), London: Sage.

—— (1994) *Meaningful Relationships*, London: Sage.

—— (1995) Repelling the study of attraction, *The Psychologist* 8 (2), 60–3.

Duck, S.W. and Wright, P. (1993) Reexamining gender differences in same-gender friendships: a close look at two kinds of data, *Sex Roles* 28, 709–27.

Durkin, K. (1995) *Developmental Social Psychology*, Oxford: Blackwell.

Ebbesen, E.B., Kjos, G.L. and Konecni, V.J. (1976) Spatial ecology: its effects on the choice of friends and enemies, *Journal of Experimental Social Psychology* 12, 505–18.

Farr, W. (1975) Marriage and mortality, in N. Humphreys (ed.), *Vital Statistics: A Memorial Volume of Selections from the Reports and Writings of William Farr*, Metuchen, NJ: Scarecrow Press. (Original work published 1885.)

Feingold, A. (1988) Matching for attractiveness in romantic partners and same-sex friends: a meta-analysis and theoretical critique, *Psychological Bulletin* 104, 226–35.

Festinger, L. (1954) A theory of social comparison processes, *Human Relations* 7, 117–40.

Festinger, L., Schachter, S. and Back , K.W. (1950) *Social Pressures in Informal Groups: A Study of Human Factors in Housing*, New York: Harper.

Finch, J. and Mason, J. (1993) *Negotiating Family Responsibilities*, London: Routledge.

Fincham, F.D. (1997) Understanding marriage: from fish scales to milliseconds, *The Psychologist* 10 (12) (December).

Flanagan, C. (1999) *Early Socialisation: Sociability and Attachment*, London: Routledge.

Fox, S. (1980) Situational determinants in affiliation, *European Journal of Social Psychology* 10, 303–7.

French, J.P.R. jun. and Raven, B.H. (1959) The bases of social power, in D.Cartwright (ed.), *Studies in Social Power*, Ann Arbor: University of Michigan Press.

Gibson, H.B. (1992) *The Emotional and Sexual Lives of Older People: A Manual for Professionals*, New York: Chapman and Hall.

Glenn, N.D. (1989) Duration of marriage, family consumption, and marital happiness, *National Journal of Sociobiology* 3, 3–24.

Gold, J.A., Ryckman, R.M. and Moseley, N.R. (1984) Romantic mood induction and attraction to a dissimilar other: is love blind?, *Personality and Social Psychology* 37, 1179–85.

Goleman, D. (1990) Support groups may do more in cancer than relieve the mind, *New York Times*, 18 October.

Goodwin, R. (1995) Personal relationships across cultures, *The Psychologist* 8 (2) (February), 73–5.

Gouaux, C. (1971) Induced affective states and interpersonal attraction, *Journal of Personality and Social Psychology* 20, 37–43.

Gove, W.R. (1979) The relationship between sex roles, marital status and mental illness, *Social Forces* 51, 34–44.

Gupta, U. and Singh, P. (1982) An exploratory study of love and liking and types of marriage, *Indian Journal of Applied Psychology* 19, 92–7.

Hagen, R. and Kahn, A. (1975) Discrimination against competent women. Paper presented at meeting of Midwestern Psychological Association, Chicago.

Harlow, H.F. (1958) The nature of love, *American Psychologist* 13, 673–85.

Harrison, A.A. (1977) Mere exposure, in L. Berkowitz (ed.), *Advances in Experimental Social Psychology* (vol. 10), New York: Academic Press.

Harry, J. (1983) Gay male and lesbian relationships, in E. Macklin and R. Rubin (eds), *Contemporary Families and Alternative Lifestyles: Handbook on Research and Theory*, London: Sage.

Hartup, W.W. (1992) *Friendships and Their Developmental Significance*, in M. McCurk (ed.), *Childhood Social Development: Contemporary Perspectives*, Hove, Sussex: Erlbaum.

Hatfield, E. and Rapson, R.L. (1987) Passionate love: new directions in research, in W.H. Jones and D. Perlman (eds), *Advances in Personal Relationships* (vol. 1), Greenwich, CT: JAI Press, 109–39.

Hatfield, E. and Walster, G.W. (1978) *A New Look at Love*, Reading, MA: Addison-Wesley.

Hatfield, E., Greenberger, E., Traupmann, J. and Lambert, P. (1982) Equity and sexual satisfaction in recently married couples, *Journal of Sex Research* 18, 18–32.

Hatfield, E., Traupmann, J., Sprecher, S., Utne, M. and Hay, J. (1985) Equity and intimate relations: recent research, in W. Ickles (ed.), *Compatible and Incompatible Relationships*, New York: Springer-Verlag.

Hayduk, L.A. (1983) Personal space: where we now stand, *Psychological Bulletin* 94, 293–335.

Hazan, C. and Shaver, P. (1987) Romantic love conceptualized as an attachment process, *Journal of Personality and Social Psychology* 52, 511–24.

Hazan, C. and Shaver, P. (1990) Love and work: an attachment-theoretical perspective, *Journal of Personality and Social Psychology* 59, 270–80.

Hazan, C., Hutt, M.J. and Markus, H. (1991) Continuity and change in inner working models of attachment, unpublished manuscript, Department of Human Development, Cornell University.

Heine, S. and Lehman, D.R. (1995) Cultural variation in unrealistic optimism: does the West feel more invulnerable than the East?, *Journal of Personality and Social Psychology* 68, 595–607.

Hendrick, C. and Hendrick, S. (1989) Research on love: does it measure up?, *Journal of Personality and Social Psychology* 56, 784–94.

Hendrick, C., Hendrick, S.S., Foote, F.H. and Slapion-Foote, M.J. (1984) Do men and women love differently?, *Journal of Social and Personal Relationships* 1, 177–95.

Hill, R. (1970) *Family Development in Three Generations*, Cambridge, MA: Schenkman.

Hofstede, G. (1984) *Culture's Consequences*, Beverley Hills, CA: Sage.

Homans, G. C. (1961) *Social Behaviour*, New York: Harcourt, Brace & World.

Hsu, F. (1971) Filial piety in Japan and China, *Journal of Comparative Family Studies* 2, 67–74.

Hu, Y. and Goldman, N. (1990) Mortality differentials by marital status: an international comparison, *Demography* 27, 233–50.

Huston, M. and Schwartz, P. (1995) The relationships of lesbian and gay men, in J.T. Wood and S.W. Duck (eds), *Under-studied Relationships*, London: Sage.

Johnson, D.J. and Rusbult, C.E. (1989) Resisting temptation: devaluation of alternative partners as a means of maintaining commitment in close relationships, *Journal of Personality and Social Psychology* 57, 967–80.

Kendel, D. (1978) Similarity in real-life adolescent friendship pairs, *Journal of Personality and Social Psychology* 36, 306–12.

Kenrick, D.T. and Johnson, G.A. (1979) Interpersonal attraction in adverse environments: a problem for the classical conditioning paradigm?, *Journal of Personality and Social Psychology* 37, 572–9.

Kenrick, D.T. and Trost, M.R., (1989) A reproductive exchange model of heterosexual relationships, in C. Hendrick (ed.), *Close Relationships. Review of Personality and Social Psychology*, Newbury Park, CA: Sage, 10.

Kerckhoff, A.C. and Davis, K.E. (1962) Value consensus and need complementarity in mate selection, *American Sociological Review* 27, 295–303.

Kirkpatrick, L.A. and Hazan, C. (1994) Attachment styles and close relationships: a four-year prospective study, *Personal Relationships* 1, 123–42.

Kitzinger, C. and Coyle, A. (1995) Lesbian and gay couples: speaking of difference, *The Psychologist* 8 (2) 64–9.

Klinger, E. (1977) Meaning and void: inner experience and the incentives in people's lives, Minneapolis: University of Minnesota Press.

Kulik, J.A. and Mahler, H.I.M. (1989) Effects of preoperative roommate assignment on preoperative anxiety and recovery from coronary-bypass surgery, *Health Psychology* 6, 525–44.

Kurdek, L.A. (1994) Areas of conflict for gay, lesbian and heterosexual couples: what couples agree about influences relationship satisfaction, *Journal of Marriage and the Family* 56, 297–313.

La Gaipa, J.J. (1982 'Rituals of disengagement', in S.W. Duck (ed.), *Personal Relationships 4: Dissolving Personal Relationships*, London: Academic Press.

Leary, M.R., Rogers, P.A., Canfield, R.W. and Coe, C. (1986) Boredom in interpersonal encounters: antecedents and social implications, *Journal of Personality and Social Psychology* 51(5), 968–75.

Lee, J.A. (1973) *Colours of Love*, Toronto: New Press.

Leigh, G.K., Homan, T.B. and Burr, W.R. (1987) Some confusions and exclusions of the SVR theory of dyadic pairing: a response to Murstein, *Journal of Marriage and the Family* 49, 933–7.

Leonard, R.L. jun. (1975) Self concept and attraction for similar and dissimilar others, *Journal of Personality and Social Psychology* 31, 926–9.

Lever, J. (1978) Sex differences in the complexity of children's play and games, *American Sociological Review* 43, 471–83.

Levinger, G. (1976) A social psychological perspective on marital dissolution, *Journal of Social Issues* 32 (1), 21–47.

—— (1980) Toward the analysis of close relationships, *Journal of Experimental Social Psychology* 16, 510–44.

—— (1983) Development and change, in H.H. Kelley, E. Berscheid, A. Christensen, J.H. Harvey, T.L. Huston, G. Levinger, E. McClintock, L.A. Peplau ad D.R. Peterson (eds), *Close Relationships*, New York: Freeman.

Levinger, G., Senn, D.J. and Jorgensen, B.W. (1970) Progress toward permanence in courtship: a test of Kerchoff–Davis hypothesis, *Sociometry* 33, 427–43.

Levitt, M.J. (1991) Attachments and close relationships: a life-span perspective, in J.L. Gewirtz and W.M. Kurtines (eds), *Interaction with Attachment*, Hillsdale, NJ: Erlbaum.

Linton, R. (1936) *The Study of Man*, New York: Appleton-Century.

Lloyd, S.A., Cate, R.M. and Henton, J.M. (1984) Predicting premarital relationship stability: a methodological refinement, *Journal of Marriage and the Family* 46, 71–76.

McGhee, P.M. (1996) Make or break? The psychology of relationship dissatisfaction and breakdown, *Psychology Review* 2 (4), 27–30.

McKillip, J. and Riedel, S.L. (1983) External validity of matching on physical attractiveness for same and opposite sex couples, *Journal of Applied Social Psychology* 13, 328–37.

McWhirter, D.P. and Mattison, A.M. (1984) *The Male Couple*, Englewood Cliffs, NJ: Prentice-Hall.

Mastekassa, A. (1992) Marriage and psychological well-being: some evidence on selection into marriage, *Journal of Marriage and the Family* 54, 901–11.

Miell, D. and Crogham, R. (1996) Examining the wider context of social relationships, in D. Miell and R. Dallos, *Social Interaction and Personal Relationships*, Milton Keynes: Open University Press, 267–318.

Moghaddem, F.M., Taylor, D.M. and Wright, S.C. (1993) *Social*

Psychology in Cross-cultural Perspective, New York: W.H. Freeman & Co.

Moreland, R.L. and Beach S.R. (1992) Exposure effects in the classroom: The development of affinity among students, *Journal of Experimental Social Psychology* 28, 255–76.

Murstein, B.I. (1970) Stimulus–value–role: a theory of marital choice, *Journal of Marriage and the Family* 32, 465–81.

—— (1974) *Love, Sex and Marriage Through the Ages*, New York: Springer.

—— (1976) *Who Will Marry Whom? Theories and Research in Marital Choice*, New York: Springer-Verlag.

Murstein, B.I., Merighi, J.R. and Vyse, S.A. (1991) Love styles in the United States and France: a cross-cultural comparison, *Journal of Social and Clinical Psychology* 10, 37–46.

Nardi, P.M. and Sherrod, D. (1994) Friendship in the lives of gay men and lesbians, *Journal of Social and Personal Relationships* 11, 185–99.

Nehamow, L. and Lawton, M.P. (1975) Similarity and propinquity in friendship formation, *Journal of Personality and Social Psychology* 32, 205–13.

Newcomb, T.M. (1961) *The Acquaintance Process*, New York: Holt, Rinehart & Winston.

Nichols, M. (1990) Lesbian relationships: implications for the study of sexuality and gender, in D.P. McWhirter, S.A. Sanders and J.M. Reinisch (eds), *Homosexuality/Heterosexuality: The Kinsey Scale and Current Research*, New York: Oxford University Press, 350–64.

Novak, D.W. and Lerner, M.J. (1968) Rejection as a consequence of perceived similarity, *Journal of Personality and Social Psychology* 9, 147–52.

Nuckolls, K.B., Cassell, J. and Kaplin, B.H. (1972) Psychosocial assets, life crisis and the prognosis of pregnancy, *American Journal of Epidemiology* 95, 431–41.

O'Leary, K.D. and Smith, D.A. (1991) Marital interaction, *Annual Review of Psychology* 42, 191–212.

Pataki, S.P., Shapiro, C. and Clark, M.S. (1994) Children's acquisition of appropriate norms for friendship and acquaintances, *Journal of Social and Personal Relations* 11, 427–42.

Pennington, D. (1986) *Essential Social Psychology*, London: Edward Arnold.

Peplau, L.A. and Gordon, S.L. (1983). The intimate relationships of lesbians and gay men, in E.R. Allegier and N.R. McCormick (eds), *Gender Roles and Sexual Behaviour: The Changing Boundaries*, Palo Alto, CA: Mayfield.

Peplau, L.A., Cochran, S., Rook K. and Padesky, C. (1978) Loving women: attachment and autonomy in lesbian relationships, *Journal of Social Issues* 34, 7–27.

Peterson, D.R. (1983) Conflict, in H.H. Kelley, *Close Relationships*, New York: Freeman.

Pineo, P.C. (1961) Disenchantment in the later years of marriage, *Journal of Marriage and Family Living* 23, 3–11.

Prins, K.S., Buunk, A.P. and Van Yperen, N.W. (1992) Equity, normative disapproval and extramarital sex, *Journal of Social and Personal Relationships* 10, 39–53.

Quindlen, A. (1992). No closet space, *New York Times*, 27 May, P.A11.

Rawlins, W. K. (1992) *Friendship Matters*, Hawthorne, NY: Aldine de Gruyter.

Reis, H.T., Senchak, M. and Solomon, B. (1985) Sex differences in the intimacy of social interaction: further examination of potential explanations, *Journal of Personality and Social Psychology* 48, 1204–17.

Reitch, J.W. and Zautra, A. (1981) Life events and personal causation: some relationships with satisfaction and distress, *Journal of Personality and Social Psychology* 41, 1002–12.

Rosenbaum, M.E. (1986) The repulsion hypothesis: on the non-development of relationships, *Journal of Personality and Social Psychology* 50, 729–36.

Rubin, Z. (1970) Measurement of romantic love, *Journal of Personality and Social Psychology* 16, 265–73.

—— (1973) *Liking and Loving*, New York: Holt, Rinehart and Winston.

Rusbult, C.E. (1983) A longitudinal test of the investment model. The development (and deterioration) of satisfaction and commitment in heterosexual involvement, *Journal of Personality and Social Psychology* 45, 101–17.

Rusbult, C.E. and Martz, J.M. (1995) Remaining in an abusive relationship: an investment model of nonvoluntary dependence, *Personality and Social Psychology Bulletin* 21, 558–71.

Rusbult, C.E. and Zembrodt, I.M. (1983) Responses to dissatisfaction in romantic involvements: a multidimensional scaling analysis, *Journal of Personality and Social Psychology* 43, 1230–42.

Rusbult, C.E., Zembrodt, I.M. and Gunn, L.K. (1982) Exit, voice, and neglect: responses to dissatisfaction in romantic involvements, *Journal of Personality and Social Psychology* 43, 1230–42.

Rusbult, C.E., Farrell, D., Rogers, G. and Mainous, A.G. (1988) Impact of exchange variables on exit, voice, loyalty, and neglect: An integrative model of responses to declining job satisfaction, *Academy of Management Journal* 31, 599–627.

Sapadin, L.A. (1988) Friendship and gender: perspectives of professional men and women, *Journal of Social and Personal Relationships* 5 (4), 387–403.

Sardar, Z. (1999) Why I didn't choose my wife, *New Statesman*, 1 May, 16–17.

Scanzoni, J. (1979) *Sex Roles, Women's Work, and Marital Conflict,* Boston, MA: D.C. Heath.

Schachter, S. (1959) *The Psychology of Affiliation: Experimental Studies of the Source of Gregariousness*, Stanford, CA: Stanford University Press.

Segal, M.W. (1974) Alphabet and attraction: an unobstrusive measure of the effect of propinquity in a field setting, *Journal of Personality and Social Psychology* 30, 654–7.

Shaver, P. and Buhrmester, D. (1983) Loneliness, sex-role orientation and group life: a social needs perspective, in P.B. Paulus (ed.), *Basic Group Processes*, New York: Springer-Verlag.

Shaver, P., Hazan, C. and Bradshaw, D. (1988) Love as attachment: the integration of three behavioural systems, in R.J. Sternberg and M.L. Barnes (eds), *The Psychology of Love*, New Haven, CT: Yale University Press, 68–99.

Sherrod, D. (1989) The influence of gender on same-sex friendships, in C. Hendrick (ed.), *Review of Personality and Social Psychology: Vol. 10 Close Relationships*, Newbury Park, CA: Sage, 164–86.

Sigall, H. and Aronson, E. (1969) Liking for an evaluation as a function of her physical attractiveness and nature of the evaluation, *Journal of Experimental Social Psychology* 5, 93–100.

Silverman, I. (1971) Physical attractiveness, *Sexual Behaviour*, 22–25 September.

Simpson, J.A. (1990) Influence of attachment styles on romantic relationships, *Journal of Personality and Social Psychology* 59, 971–80.

Singh, D. (1993) Adaptive significance of female attractiveness: role of waist-to-hip ratio, *Journal of Personality and Social Psychology* 65, 293–307.

Smeaton, G., Byrne, D. and Murnen, S.K. (1989) The repulsion hypothesis revisited; similarity irrelevance or dissimilarity bias?, *Journal of Personality and Social Psychology* 56, 54–9.

Smith, P.B. and Bond, M.H. (1993) *Social Psychology Across Cultures*, Cambridge: Harvester-Wheatsheaf.

Sprecher, S., Aron, A., Hatfield, E., Cortese, A., Potapova, E. and Levitskaya, A. (1994) Love American style, Russian style and Japanese style, *Personal Relationships* 1, 349–69.

Stephen, T. (1985) Taking communication seriously: a reply to Murstein, *Journal of Marriage and the Family*, 47, 937–8.

Sternberg, R.J. and Barnes, M.L. (1988) *The Psychology of Love*, London: Yale University Press.

Stiles, D., Gibbon, J., Hardardottir, S. and Schnellmann, J. (1987) The ideal man or woman as described by young adolescents in Iceland and the United States, *Sex Roles* 17, 313–20.

Sullivan, H.S. (1953) *The Interpersonal Theory of Psychiatry*, New York: Norton.

Surra, C.A. and Huston, T.L. (1987) Mate selection as a social transition, in D. Perlman and S. Duck (eds), *Intimate Relationships: Development, Dynamics and Deterioration*, Newbury Park, CA: Sage Publications, 88–120.

Thibaut, J.W. and Kelley, H.H. (1959) *The Social Psychology of Groups*, New York: Wiley.

Tolstedt, B.E. and Stokes, J.P. (1984) Self-disclosure, intimacy, and the depenetration process, *Journal of Personality and Social Psychology* 46, 84–90.

Triandis, H.C., McCusker, C. and Hui, C.H. (1990) Multimethod probes of individualism and collectivism, *Journal of Personality and Social Psychology* 59, 1006–20.

Trivers, R.L. (1972) Parental investment and sexual selection, in B. Campbell (ed.), *Sexual Selection and the Descent of Man*, Chicago: Aldine-Atherton, 136–79.

Unger, R. and Crawford, M. (1992) *Women and Gender: A Feminist Psychology*, New York: McGraw-Hill.

Veitch, R. and Griffith, W. (1976) Good news, bad news: affective and interpersonal effects, *Journal of Applied Social Psychology* 6, 69–75.

Waller, W.W. and Hill, R. (1951) *The Family, a Dynamic Interpretation*, New York: Warner Books.

Walster, E. and Walster, G.W. (1978) *A New Look at Love*, Reading, MA: Addison-Wesley.

Walster, E., Aronson, V., Abrahams, D. and Rottmann, L. (1966) Importance of physical attractiveness in dating behaviour, *Journal of Personality and Social Psychology* 4, 508–16.

Warr, P. (1983) Work, jobs and employment, *Bulletin of the British Psychological Society* 36, 305–11.

Winch, R.F. (1958) *Mate Selection: A Study of Complementary Needs*, New York: Harper & Row.

Wright, P.H. (1982) Men's friendships, women's friendships and the alleged inferiority of the latter, *Sex Roles* 8, 1–20.

Yinin, Y., Goldenberg, J. and Neeman, R. (1977) On the relationship structure of residence and formation of friendship, *Psychological Reports* 40, 761–2.

Zajonc, R.B. (1968) Attitudinal effects of mere exposure, *Journal of Personality and Social Psychology* 8, 1–29.

Index